READING THE BIBLE

WITH

MARTIN LUTHER

AN INTRODUCTORY GUIDE

TIMOTHY J. WENGERT

Baker Academic
a division of Baker Publishing Group
Grand Rapids, Michigan

© 2013 by Timothy J. Wengert

Published by Baker Academic
a division of Baker Publishing Group
P.O. Box 6287, Grand Rapids, MI 49516-6287
www.bakeracademic.com

Printed in the United States of America

All rights reserved. No part of this publication may be reproduced, stored in a retrieval system, or transmitted in any form or by any means—for example, electronic, photocopy, recording—without the prior written permission of the publisher. The only exception is brief quotations in printed reviews.

Library of Congress Cataloging-in-Publication Data
Wengert, Timothy J.
    Reading the Bible with Martin Luther : an introductory guide / Timothy J. Wengert.
        pages cm
    Includes bibliographical references and index.
    ISBN 978-0-8010-4917-0 (pbk.)
    1. Luther, Martin, 1483–1546. 2. Bible—Criticism, interpretation, etc. I. Title.
BR333.5.B5W46 2013
220.6092—dc23   2013016563

Unless indicated otherwise, Scripture translations are those of the author.

Scripture quotations labeled KJV are from the King James Version of the Bible.

Scripture quotations labeled NRSV are from the New Revised Standard Version of the Bible, copyright © 1989, by the Division of Christian Education of the National Council of the Churches of Christ in the United States of America. Used by permission. All rights reserved.

Translations of Luther's 1535 Galatians commentary are from *Luther's Works Vol. 26* © 1963, 1991 Concordia Publishing House. Used with permission. www.cph.org

In keeping with biblical principles of creation stewardship, Baker Publishing Group advocates the responsible use of our natural resources. As a member of the Green Press Initiative, our company uses recycled paper when possible. The text paper of this book is composed in part of post-consumer waste.

13 14 15 16 17 18 19   7 6 5 4 3 2 1

Contents

Abbreviations

Ap	Apology of the Augsburg Confession
BC	*The Book of Concord*. Edited by Robert Kolb and Timothy J. Wengert. Minneapolis: Fortress, 2000.
CA	Augsburg Confession
CR	*Corpus Reformatorum: Philippi Melanthonis opera quae supersunt omnia*. Edited by Karl Bretschneider and Heinrich Bindseil. 28 vols. Halle: A. Schwetschke & Sons, 1834–60.
LC	Large Catechism
LW	*Luther's Works* [American edition]. Edited by Jaroslav Pelikan and Helmut T. Lehmann. 55 vols. Philadelphia: Fortress; St. Louis: Concordia, 1955–86.
MBW	*Melanchthons Briefwechsel: Kritische und kommentierte Gesamtausgabe: Regesten*. Edited by Heinz Scheible. 12+ vols. Stuttgart-Bad Cannstatt: Frommann-Holzboog, 1977–. The numbers following MBW refer to the number of the letters.
SC	Small Catechism
StLA	*Dr. Martin Luthers Sämmtliche Schriften*. Edited by Johann Georg Walch. 2nd ed. 23 vols. St. Louis: Concordia, 1892–1910.
Texte	*Melanchthons Briefwechsel: Kritische und kommentierte Gesamtausgabe: Texte*. Edited by Heinz Scheible et al. 11+

vols. Stuttgart-Bad Cannstatt: Frommann-Holzboog, 1991–.
See also MBW above.

WA *Luthers Werke: Kritische Gesamtausgabe [Schriften].* 65 vols. Weimar: H. Böhlau, 1883–1993.

WA DB *Luthers Werke: Kritische Gesamtausgabe: Bibel.* 12 vols. Weimar: H. Böhlau, 1906–61.

WA Br *Luthers Werke: Kritische Gesamtausgabe: Briefwechsel.* 18 vols. Weimar: H. Böhlau, 1930–85.

WA TR *Luthers Werke: Kritische Gesamtausgabe: Tischreden.* 6 vols. Weimar: H. Böhlau, 1912–21.

Preface

Can today's Christians read the Bible with Martin Luther? Or, more accurately, can they hear God's Word with Martin Luther? The answer to these questions can be a resounding yes! Reading and listening to the Bible with Luther, however, challenges our own approaches to Scripture, forcing us to move away from both more fundamentalistic and more liberal methods of biblical interpretation. The five essays in this book outline what Luther offers to Christians and discover fresh approaches to Scripture in which God may speak anew.

We begin in chapter 1 with one of the most contested subjects not only in American Lutheranism but also among other Protestant churches: the authority of the Bible. Here, in contrast to a (nonbiblical) insistence on an "inerrant and infallible" text, Luther's treatment of the book of James, clouded by centuries of misconstrual, may help guide us to hear anew the authoritative center of Scripture as Luther experienced it: "*Was Christum treibet*" (what pushes Christ). This interpretive key to Scripture, best summarized by the phrase *solus Christus* (Christ alone), contrasts with Luther's reticence concerning and occasional rejection of the phrase *sola Scriptura* (Scripture alone), which some later Christians invoked to support more literalistic approaches to Scripture. Indeed, Luther was far more interested in God's

Word *proclaimed* and not merely shut up in a book. The church, he once said, is a mouth house, not a quill house.

Chapter 2 investigates the related question of method, focusing on the approach shared by both Martin Luther and his close colleague Philip Melanchthon—namely, distinguishing law and gospel. Here we will learn that this distinction, far from being simply a technique for separating commands from promises, has specifically to do with how God's Word affects its hearers. As law, God's Word keeps order and restrains sin in this world (what Melanchthon labeled the civil or "first use" of the law), and it reveals sin and puts the old creature to death (the theological or "second use" of the law). As gospel, God's Word declares forgiveness and brings to life the new creature of faith. Because a "third use" of the law, coined by Melanchthon and emphasized by John Calvin, figured in later Lutheran debates of the sixteenth century, this chapter will also examine this "use" of the law so that readers may discover what Lutherans, at least, meant by such a use—namely, the first and second uses of the law applied to believers.

The third chapter then takes up the central interpretative tool for hearing God's Word in Scripture: the inherent weakness of the text, which always witnesses to the concomitant weakness of Christ crucified. Here, more than anywhere else, Luther's interpretation of Scripture diverges from other approaches prevalent then and now. Whereas the old creature lusts after "the kingdom, power, and glory" and tries to turn Scripture into a book that meets its addiction to control, God comes in the weakness of words—mirroring the weakness of the Word made flesh—and by that very weakness wrests control from us and makes us believers. Closely related to Scripture's weakness in Reformation thought is the insistence that Scripture has a center, most clearly defined in Romans, and that each biblical book also has a focal point from which it may be read.

The fourth chapter looks at another important and disputed area of Luther's biblical thought: his approach to ethics. This essay investigates four important aspects of Luther's ethical thinking that, while not exhaustive, provide an important outline to some themes neglected in ethical deliberations today. Luther and Melanchthon championed an approach to equity and balance that called into question the merciless application of law (even God's law) in moral considerations. This concern went hand in hand with his notion of the "bound conscience" and provided him with a basis on which to corral the human potential for coercive legalism that so often mars Christian ethics and obscures the central role of pastoral concerns. Connected with these two matters is the central place of faith in Christ, which properly norms all Christian behavior and from which all Christian conduct arises. Finally, Luther's ethic was hardly individualistic but arose within the Christian community.

The final chapter looks at a single example of Luther's exegesis to give readers a better sense of how many of the principles outlined in the earlier chapters actually function. This chapter began as a presentation for a conference at St. Andrews University in Scotland. It concentrates on Galatians 3:6–14, a particularly important passage for Luther's understanding of law and Christ's atoning death. One can see here just how the authority of a passage, its effect, and its central, foolish point converge to provide Luther with a text's meaning. By looking at Luther's commentaries on Galatians from 1519 and 1535, readers will also get some sense of the variety and continuity in Luther's approach to Scripture and can consider this chapter simply an invitation to delve deeper into Luther's own commentaries and sermons on the Bible.

Special thanks are due to Pastor Irving Sandberg, who was instrumental in inviting me to speak before the rostered leaders of the Northeast Iowa Synod of the Evangelical Lutheran Church in America (ELCA) on this topic. From those original talks the first three chapters arose. The fourth chapter began as an address to the pastors of the New England Synod of the ELCA. In both cases, the questions and responses of those leaders have shaped the final product. Portions of the fourth chapter regarding the orders of creation and the "bound conscience" began as reflections written for the task force for the ELCA Studies on Sexuality, of which I was a member from 2002 to 2009. I am very much indebted to the profound conversations about sexual ethics that arose in that task force. In any case, of course, all of the statements here are my own.

Timothy J. Wengert
Holy Cross Day, 2012

1

Authority

Putting James in Its Place

This book examines three matters involving the uniquely Lutheran way of viewing Scripture—Luther's understanding of authority, method, and interpretation—before concluding with a brief look at the complicated question of Luther's approach to ethics and a detailed analysis of his interpretation of a single biblical text. This first chapter discusses the issue of authority, the issue about which Luther says the least but for which he is, especially among non-Lutherans, the best known. The next chapter considers the Lutheran method of law and gospel. The third chapter looks at the heart of actual Lutheran biblical interpretation: the cross. The final two chapters investigate specific examples of Luther's approach to the Bible at work in ethics and in his interpretation of Galatians.

James and Straw

If one says the words *Luther* and *James* in the same sentence, Lutherans groan and non-Lutheran Protestants roll their eyes. It may come as a surprise, but not much had been written about Luther and James (at least in English) until a PhD student at The Lutheran Theological Seminary at Philadelphia wrote his dissertation on a closely related topic. In a study of English Puritan interpretations of James, Derek Cooper discovered that even if these divines of the mid-seventeenth century knew nothing else about Martin Luther, they at least knew this: he did not like James and had tried to kick it out of the canon or at least stick it in an appendix.[1] Moreover, they all knew that he called it an epistle of straw.

Before we can use what Luther wrote to help us unravel the question of authority, we need to know the facts. Luther talked about James in two places in his translation of the New Testament, published in September 1522: in the general preface to the New Testament and in the specific preface to the books of James and Jude. But what few realize is that in 1534, while retaining what he said in the preface to James and Jude, he deleted his comments about James in the general preface to the New Testament from the first and every subsequent edition of the complete Bible, and that after 1539 the same comments were removed from separate printings of the New Testament. What did he write?

At the end of his 1522 preface to the New Testament, Luther included a section entitled "Which Are the Correct and Purest Books of the New Testament." On the basis of criteria that he had introduced earlier in the preface, Luther concluded that the best books are the Gospel of John, Paul's Letters (chief among them Romans), and 1 Peter. He suggested to his readers that they read these first and most often until they became their daily bread: "For in these you will not find much description of Christ's works and miracles, but instead you will find depicted in a masterly way how faith in Christ overcomes sin, death, and hell and gives life, righteousness, and salvation, which is the proper meaning of *gospel*, as you have heard."[2]

---

1. Derek Cooper, "The Ecumenical Exegete: Thomas Manton's Commentary on James in Relation to Its Protestant Predecessors, Contemporaries and Successors" (PhD diss., The Lutheran Theological Seminary at Philadelphia, 2008), now published in a revised edition as *Thomas Manton: A Guided Tour of the Life and Thought of a Puritan Pastor* (Phillipsburg, NJ: P&R, 2011). The following paragraphs are based on Cooper's work.

2. WA DB 6:10, 15–19 (=LW 35:362). All translations are the author's own, unless otherwise noted.

Well and good! For people not used to reading the New Testament and perhaps bewildered by its complexity, Luther went for the gold. But then he added these words:

> In sum, St. John's Gospel and his first epistle; St. Paul's letters, especially the ones to the Romans, Galatians, and Ephesians; and St. Peter's first epistle are all books that show you Christ, and they all teach what is necessary and salutary for you to know, even if you do not see or hear any other book or teaching. It is for this reason that James's epistle is in comparison a real strawy epistle, for it has no evangelical character about it.[3]

Note a few things here. First, Luther placed James alongside the other New Testament authors, whom (unlike James) he calls saints. Second, his main point of contrast was that these books "show you Christ." This was really Luther's only criterion for judging Scripture, so that in contrast he said about James that it "has no evangelical character about it." By that he meant that it preached law, not gospel. Third, he used the word "straw" not as some sort of strange German insult but as an echo of Paul's picture in 1 Corinthians 3:12 about building on the foundation of Christ with either straw or gold and precious stones. James builds on the foundation all right, but he uses only straw, in contrast to the gold standard of John, Paul, and Peter.

In the preface to James itself, which remained unaltered in later editions of Luther's translation, Luther provided a bit more detail but also some real surprises. First, Luther revealed in the very first sentence something that many people today have forgotten: that the ancient church was also very skeptical about James: "although it was rejected by the ancient church," he began.[4] What Luther did not mention is that he was also not the only person in the sixteenth century to question the authorship of James. In annotations on the Greek New Testament, no less a scholar than Erasmus of Rotterdam had done the same. On the basis of Erasmus's arguments, Tommaso de Vio (better known to us as Cardinal Cajetan, who interviewed Luther in Augsburg in 1518) also called the authorship and authority

3. WA DB 6:10, 29–35 (=LW 35:362).
4. WA DB 7:384, 3–4 (=LW 35:395).

of James into question. So Luther was actually one humanist scholar among several who raised questions about James's authenticity—as had several in the ancient church as well.[5] Luther was not so much going out on a limb as revisiting some old debates in the church with a new critical eye.

If discovering that others also questioned James's authority comes as a surprise, what Luther said next is downright shocking: "I praise James and hold it to be a good writing because it does not propose human teachings but drives God's law hard."[6] James preaches *God's* law, not the silly *human* teachings so beloved by the papacy (and, it turns out, by a lot of people who want to defend James's canonical authority). Luther praised James! Despite this good review, Luther then entered the actual debate about the apostolicity of James, stating at the outset that this was simply his own opinion and that others could differ with him on this matter (no papal decree, this!). He gave two reasons for his misgivings, the first of which was new to the debate and the second of which only tangentially arose out of traditional objections to the book. He then followed that with a theory about the book's composition.

Luther's first reason for rejecting James was that "it is completely contrary to St. Paul and all other Scripture in that it attributes justification to works and saying that Abraham was justified by his works because he offered his son, despite the fact that St. Paul teaches the opposite in Romans 4, citing Genesis 15 that he is justified by faith

5. The word *humanist*, as used in the sixteenth century, did not describe *secularists* as in today's English usage but an intellectual movement, begun in Italy during the Renaissance, that emphasized writing and speaking polished Latin and reading good literature (*bonae litterae*, "good letters") and returning to the earliest sources in the humanities, theology, medicine, and law (*ad fontes*, "to the fonts [sources]"). As Helmar Junghans and others have shown, Luther was strongly influenced by humanism. See Helmar Junghans, *Der junge Luther und die Humanisten* (Weimar: Böhlaus Nachfolger, 1984). In English, see his "Luther's Development from Biblical Humanist to Reformer," in Helmar Junghans, *Martin Luther in Two Centuries* (St. Paul: Lutheran Brotherhood Foundation Reformation Library, 1992), 1–14. Ancient questions about this epistle were preserved in Eusebius, *The History of the Church from Christ to Constantine*, trans. G. A. Williamson (Harmondsworth, UK: Penguin, 1965; repr., Minneapolis: Augsburg, 1975), 103 (II, xxiii, 25) and 134 (III, xxv, 3).

6. WA DB 7:384, 4–6 (=LW 35:395).

alone, a text that comes before the sacrifice of Isaac."[7] What most folks do not remember is that Luther made clear that he was talking about the literal texts of Paul and James, which indeed contradict one another. However, he knew that some people—probably some in his own inner circle—tried to explain the contradiction away. So he added, "Although this epistle may perchance be helped and an explanatory gloss for justification by works may be found, yet one cannot protect it from the fact that it connects the saying of Moses in Genesis 15 to works," when that was not what Moses intended at all.[8] This kind of weakness, he concluded, shows that it was not apostolic. Thus, the issue for Luther was not so much James's teaching about works, which could be made to agree with Paul, but its clumsy misuse of Scripture.

Luther's second suspicion about James could be summarized in a single German phrase: apostolicity has to do with "*Was Christum treibet*," whatever emphasizes, drives, or pushes Christ.[9] Luther rejected the apostolicity of this letter,

> second, because it tries to teach Christians and yet does not mention even once with any teaching of any length the suffering, the resurrection, or the Spirit of Christ. He mentions Christ a few times and yet does not teach anything about him but instead talks about general faith in God. Indeed, the office of a true apostle is that he preaches about Christ's suffering, resurrection, and office, and lays the foundation of this very faith, as Christ himself says in John 15, "You will bear witness to me." And in this all the correctly written holy books agree, so that they all preach and emphasize Christ. This is also the proper touchstone by which to measure all books, when a person observes whether or not they emphasize Christ. Since all Scripture reveals Christ (Rom. 3) and since Paul wants to know nothing but Christ (1 Cor. 2), whatever does not teach Christ is not apostolic, even if Peter or Paul taught it. Or again, what preaches Christ is apostolic, even if Judas, Annas, Pilate, and Herod did it.[10]

7. WA DB 7:384, 9–14 (=LW 35:396).
8. WA DB 7:384, 14–18 (=LW 35:396).
9. The German verb *treiben* is etymologically related to the English *drive* but has a wide variety of meanings around that central sense of "push" or "drive."
10. WA DB 7:384, 19–32 (=LW 35:396).

This is by far the most devastating criticism, one that no one who has read James can deny. In other words, excluding the really small letters (Jude, 2 and 3 John, Philemon), if somehow only one book of the New Testament had survived to the present, it would be virtually impossible to know anything about Christ or the Holy Spirit if all one had was James. And yet there are people who insist on reading the rest of the New Testament through this one skimpy book. Frankly, on the basis of its Christology, calling James an epistle of straw was a compliment. There is no witness to Jesus Christ, no mention of his saving crucifixion and his resurrection, and no discussion at all of the Holy Spirit. Luther's rejection of James had less to do with the Reformer's "odd" reading of Paul on justification (which many people now think was wrong anyway) than with the central biblical question of the apostolic office.

But far more useful for a discussion of the authority of Scripture is what else Luther wrote here, because he gave a remarkable way to judge not only Scripture but other Christian writings as well. Suddenly, apostolicity—that is, the debate from the ancient church over whether an apostle named James wrote James—becomes moot. If Judas wrote a book *and it pushed Christ*, then it is apostolic.[11] The same criterion Luther used to criticize his Roman opponents and the Roman papacy had now become the measuring stick and touchstone for Scripture itself.[12] Esther did not mention God, so it is a nice story but do not confuse it with the gospel.[13] In fact, one can also easily dismiss much of the pseudepigraphical literature on the basis of this criterion. But it also means that Luther has given us a tool for judging

11. This is why the recent furor over a Gospel of Judas would have seemed so silly to Luther. The primary question for an exegete following Luther's lead can never simply be "Who wrote it?" but "Does it push Christ?"

12. For Luther's criticism of the papacy, see Scott Hendrix, *Luther and the Papacy* (Philadelphia: Fortress, 1984). Whereas at the beginning of the Reformation Luther thought that the pope was being misinformed, by 1520 he was convinced that the institution of the papacy, because of its claims to authority over the church on earth and its Scriptures, had abandoned Christ's gospel of forgiveness and thus had become anti-Christian.

13. This is something Luther mentioned in passing in his debate with Erasmus over the freedom of the will. See WA 18:666, 23 (=LW 33:110), explained in detail by Heinrich Bornkamm, *Luther and the Old Testament*, trans. Eric W. and Ruth C. Gritsch (Philadelphia: Fortress, 1969), 188n391.

contemporary works. By Luther's criterion, the Left Behind series (or as I like to call it, the "Home Alone" series) is not worth a person's time, unless perhaps he or she is caught in a lake cabin during a snowstorm and has already read all of the Danielle Steele on the shelves. But even then one may prefer to use them as fuel for the fire. To use a different example, a pastor and friend of mine once perused six months' worth of the online sermons of a particularly well-known Lutheran megachurch and discovered that *not once* was Jesus' death and resurrection even mentioned. Talk about strawy preaching! And those who use every sermon to turn Jesus into simply an example to follow will fare no better.[14]

Finally, Luther examined the style and content of James. "He pushes [emphasizes] the law and its works,"[15] Luther wrote, and James did it in a very disorderly fashion. Luther suggested that either some pious Christian wrote James by stringing together some words handed down by disciples of the apostles or James consisted of a pious Christian's sermon recorded by someone else. The fact that the author had taken lines from the letters of Peter and Paul (for which Luther provided examples) proved to Luther that the author could hardly be the apostle and early martyr James but that the book had to have been written long after the apostles. Many modern exegetes agree.[16]

In sum, Luther concluded, the author wanted to protect against those who trusted in faith without giving any attention to works at all, but he just could not pull it off. He wanted to accomplish with an emphasis on the law what the apostles achieved by stressing love. For these reasons, Luther could not put this among the chief books but instead stuck it in an appendix of less important books (including Jude and Revelation). Still, he refused to criticize those who wanted to rehabilitate the book, since it did contain some really good sayings—just nothing about the Savior Jesus Christ or the Holy Spirit.

14. Thus, in an earlier section of his preface to the New Testament, Luther warned his readers, "Therefore watch out that you do not make a Moses [i.e., lawgiver] out of Christ, nor out of the Gospel a book of laws or doctrines, as has happened up until now" (WA DB 6:8, 3–4 [=LW 35:360]).

15. WA DB 7:386, 1–2 (=LW 35:396–97).

16. See, for example, Pheme Perkins, *First and Second Peter, James, and Jude* (Louisville: Westminster John Knox, 1995), 83–85, 93–95.

The Self-Authenticating Scripture

So how does this little foray into Luther's comments on James help with the topic of authority? At this point, it should be quite clear. For Luther, scriptural authority was not a precondition for faith but a result of it. His understanding of Scripture was thus just the opposite of that of many contemporary Christians in America. Luther never said, "The Bible says it, I believe it, that settles it," but just the opposite: "Because I believe in Christ, therefore I can judge all things through him" (cf. Phil. 4:13). What pushes Christ pushes me. Or, to put it another way, when Luther approached Scripture, his first and only question was (to quote an old television ad) "Where's the beef?" or, rather (to paraphrase St. Paul), "Where are the gold, pearls, diamonds, emeralds, and rubies?" Put still another way: for Luther, Scripture is self-authenticating. The Bible is God's Word because it *does* God in Christ to me, killing the old and raising the new. Luther's decision to make the *evangel*—the good news—key in judging James calls into question all forms of biblical fundamentalism. Before discussing Luther's radical insight, however, consider briefly the alternative.

Fundamentalists must start outside Scripture to authenticate it.[17] That is, they begin with a definition of truth that they then apply to the biblical text. If the Bible lives up to their definition of truth, it is true; if not, it is false. Now, their definition of truth is *apophatic*; that is, it is a definition from negation. In order to be true the Bible must *not* have two things: it must *not* contain errors and it must *not* contain falsehoods; that is, it must be *in*-errant and *in*-fallible, where the Latin prefix "in" means "not." Of course, any such definition always results in setting a standard that is humanly impossible to meet, so immediately the fundamentalist builds in some obvious caveats: individual copies of the Bible contain scribal errors; there can always be errors in transmission and interpretation. However, when it comes to questions of content, the Bible contains neither errors nor falsehoods, where the measure for both errors and falsehoods arises from human definitions brought in to judge Scripture.

17. The best book on American fundamentalism is still George M. Marsden, *Fundamentalism and American Culture: The Shaping of Twentieth Century Evangelicalism, 1870–1925*, 2nd ed. (New York: Oxford, 2006).

There is also a companion difficulty. Who says *this* collection of books is the Bible? Here is where Luther's challenge was especially worrisome and was part of the reason that Luther came in for such harsh criticism by seventeenth-century English Puritans. The Bible is clearly a historical accident. Thanks to a Jewish council in Jamnia from AD 90, a hard-to-date list from the second through fourth century (the Muratorian Canon), and the festal letter by Athanasius from AD 367, we have a canon. Add to that St. Augustine of Hippo's famous line, "I would not have believed the gospel if the authority of the church had not moved me," and Protestants are in real trouble. No matter how one slices it, Augustine seems to put the church above Scripture. First believe the church, which formed the canon; then believe the Bible. The Roman Catholic theologians debating Protestants never grew tired of pointing out the irony. The more the Protestants emphasized the authority of the Bible, the more they inadvertently proved the greater authority of the church. Of course, Augustine's comment had nothing to do with episcopal or papal authority and everything to do with the authority of the church's *witness*, the very point Luther was also making. Nevertheless, by appealing to the canon of the Bible, once again human authority authorizes Scripture.

The fact that fundamentalists so vehemently insist on Scripture's infallibility and inerrancy also has to do with a further aspect of their theology: the notion that Scripture contains two kinds of truths, verifiable and nonverifiable. The problem is simple. The *fundamentals* of the Christian faith, to use their term for it, are such things as the virgin birth, the bodily resurrection, the substitutionary theory of the atonement, along with such doctrines as the Trinity and the two natures of Christ. These cannot be verified in any scientific or logical way in Scripture but must simply be asserted. No one denies that. To vouch for Scripture's authenticity, however, there are also verifiable scientific and historical facts: creation in six days, the flood, Jonah swallowed by a whale. Were these shown to be contrary to fact, the nonverifiable truths could also no longer be trusted. That is, if the world is five billion years old, then there is no God, no Christ, and no salvation.[18]

18. This shows just how rationalistic fundamentalism finally is.

Finally, the fundamentalists' approach to Scripture arises out of law. After all, the definition of truth is a law. The logic of no errors and no falsehoods is the logic of law. The division of truth into two types is a fundamental *tenet*—that is, a law. Moreover, the acceptance of the *canon* of Scripture is a law. Now, to be sure, most laypeople in such churches, when they recite the mantra, "The Bible says it, I believe it, that settles it," are not thinking about the prior authorization of Scripture. Indeed, they leave that to—well, to whom? To their pastors and leaders who tell them what to believe, who teach them how to overcome any contradictions, and who insist on the Bible's authority. Thus, at the heart of fundamentalism, as it is currently practiced in some American churches, is nothing more than a congregational form of papalism, because the actual mantra reads, "My pastor says the Bible said it, I believe him, that settles it." That is the law!

Luther, contrary to all of this, insisted that Scripture was self-authenticating. It is God's Word because it "does God" to me.[19] James gets put into an appendix precisely because all it contains is law—God's law, mind you, but law nevertheless. It does not witness to what God is doing in Christ and therefore cannot finally *do* God to a person—that is, put the old creature to death and then bring the new to life. Or, to put it another way, God's Word makes believers in Christ out of us. When a word does not do that, no matter who the author may be, it is not God's Word and has no—or only limited—authority.

Did this put Luther over Scripture, deciding what is in and what is out? Did he, by throwing James in the trunk (or under the Reformation bus), become a Lutheran pope? No, for two reasons. First, Luther was very careful to state that this was his opinion about James and that he did not demand allegiance to it, only to the gospel. Second, Luther's position actually resulted in the very opposite. Luther's criterion, "*Was Christum treibet*" (what pushes Christ), actually put not only James but also Luther under Christ. His criterion for scriptural authority is not "*Was Lutherum treibet*" (what pushes Luther) or, worse yet, "*Was*

---

19. Gerhard Forde, *Theology Is for Proclamation* (Minneapolis: Fortress, 1990), 2–8. Forde's provocative turn of phrase, "to do God to us," seeks to avoid reducing God to attributes (static nouns) and emphasizes that what God did in Christ (die and rise again) is what God does to us: kill the old creature and raise up a new creature of faith through the Word of law and gospel.

Lutherus treibet" (what Luther pushes) but "*Was Christum treibet*" (what pushes Christ).

To put it another way, there is a claim to truth that norms Scripture, but it is the same norm that norms Luther and any interpreter of Scripture. Later Protestant scholastic theologians (but not early Lutherans) distinguished between Scripture (as an authority and norm over every other authority) and creeds and confessions (as authorities subject to scriptural authority).[20] In some ways, Scripture *is* that higher authority, but in one important way it is not. There is only one authority, and that is the crucified and risen One. Only that authority authorizes all subsequent authorities, scriptural or otherwise. "Whoever hears you, hears me" (Luke 10:16). Paul, Peter, Mary Magdalene, Luther, and one's own pastor are all normed by that very Christ. Thus, by calling James to account, Luther is also at the same time calling himself to account. If Luther starts preaching a gospel other than what he preached, let him be accursed, to paraphrase Paul's own self-cursing in Galatians 1:8–9.[21] This means that "*Was Christum treibet*" drives not just Scripture but the ministry and, in fact, the entire church. Moreover, Luther rejected both James and the papacy for the same reason: they pushed law, not Christ. The book of James was better than the papacy only because it pushed God's law; the papacy did not.

What happens to the Hebrew Scriptures? Surely, they do not explicitly push Christ, do they? Luther did not quite face the problem that we have, in that he assumed a single, divine author for both Testaments and therefore a logic that transcended both.[22] He was, for instance, convinced that the Trinity was easier to prove from the Old Testament than from the New, something that may be hard to imagine with a more historicized approach to the Bible. Modern

20. This is sometimes talked about using the Latin phrases *norma normans* and *norma normata*, respectively. See Heinrich Schmid, *The Doctrinal Theology of the Evangelical Lutheran Church*, 3rd ed., trans. Charles A. Hay and Henry E. Jacobs (Philadelphia: Lutheran Publication Society, 1876; repr., Minneapolis: Augsburg, 1961), 38–102; and Werner Elert, *The Structure of Lutheranism*, 2nd ed., trans. Walter A. Hansen (St. Louis: Concordia, 1962), 179–210.

21. This was a crucial passage in the early debates with Rome, so that Luther even used it in his letter to the emperor after the Diet of Worms in 1521. See WA Br 2:307–10 (=LW 48:203–9).

22. See Bornkamm, *Luther and the Old Testament*, 195–218.

training in Scripture, whether conservative or liberal, derives many of its insights primarily from Reformed branches of Christianity rather than from Lutheran ones. Thus, it is very hard to answer the question of the relation of the Testaments without running afoul of some very cherished notions about chronology, literary types, covenants, and, above all, salvation history. To put it most radically, Luther and those who follow his approach prefer saying that the Hebrew Scriptures, like the New Testament, gain authority when they too support Christians in their faith—that is, in their trust of God in Christ. And do they ever do that!

To understand how Luther developed his position on this question, we need to know what his options were as he commenced lecturing on the Bible in 1513 as a professor of theology at the University of Wittenberg. One of the first things he did upon entering the classroom for the first time as a doctor of the Bible was to explain the medieval *Quadriga*, or fourfold interpretative scheme for Scripture. Using the examples of Jerusalem and Babylon, Luther pointed out that each biblical text had a literal meaning (cities in the Near East), an "allegorical"[23] meaning (good or bad people), a tropological (moral) meaning (virtues and vices), and an anagogical (future-oriented) meaning (rewards and punishment). Indeed, the standard approach defined *allegoria* as anything to do with doctrine and Christ's relation to the church or the congregation of heretics (hence, with faith), *tropologia* as anything to do with the soul and God (hence, with virtues and vices and especially love), and *anagogia* as anything to do with future blessedness or judgment (and hence with hope).[24] The medieval exegetical tradition linked three Latin gerunds to these three "spiritual" interpretations of the text corresponding to the three theological virtues of faith, love, and hope—namely, *credenda* (what must be believed), *agenda* (what must be done), and *speranda* (what must be hoped for). This implied, as Gerhard Ebeling has noted, that the entire interpretive scheme emerged from the

23. In English usage, the word *allegory* is used more generally for any spiritual meanings read into a text. Here Luther was using the term quite narrowly to describe interpretations that revolve around people in the church in relation to Christ's teaching.
24. At the same time, Luther read the Old Testament text typologically—that is, as having to do chiefly with foreshadowing Christ. See below.

law.[25] What the reader had to believe, do, or hope for was the key to understanding the biblical text.

To appreciate fully how Luther developed an approach that differed from its predecessors, the work of James Samuel Preus, for years a professor of Reformation history at Indiana University, can help. His book *From Shadow to Promise*[26] argued that the breakthrough in Luther's Psalms lectures was a new way of reading the Psalms that, in one way, removed Jesus from them in order to allow him to come back. In lecturing on the Psalms from 1513 to 1515, Luther discovered what Preus termed "the faithful synagogue." Immediately before Luther, biblical interpreters had begun to argue that there were two literal senses of the Psalms: the historical-literal sense dealt with the prayers of the people of Israel, and the prophetic-literal sense read these same Psalms on Jesus' lips as prophecies of his suffering, death, and resurrection. Although some medieval commentators wanted to give equal voice to both meanings, the most important interpreter of the Psalms immediately before the Reformation, Faber Stapulensis (Jacques Lefèvre d'Étaples [ca. 1455–1536]), had argued that the historical-literal meaning was the killing letter referred to in 2 Corinthians 3:6, to be avoided at all costs in favor of the prophetic-literal, which contained the life-giving Spirit. For him, Jesus literally prayed all of the Psalms, something Luther reiterated by beginning his own lectures on the Psalms at the University of Wittenberg in 1513 with a "Preface of Jesus Christ."[27]

But somewhere in Luther's lectures on the Psalms and certainly by the time he reached Psalm 119, Preus argued, a strange thing happened. Luther discovered the believer praying for God to act, praying for Messiah to come, praying for victory over evil. Suddenly, it was not so much Jesus as God's Son praying the Psalms instead of human beings, but human beings, faithful Israel, praying to God. Just as the Israelites had prayed for God to intervene on their behalf, so too Christians prayed for God to act, not only now but also at the end of

25. Gerhard Ebeling, "The Beginnings of Luther's Hermeneutics," *Lutheran Quarterly* 7 (1993): 129–58, 315–38, 451–68.

26. James Samuel Preus, *From Shadow to Promise: Old Testament Interpretation from Augustine to the Young Luther* (Cambridge, MA: Belknap, 1969).

27. WA 3:12–13 (=LW 10:6–7).

time with the return of Christ. Indeed, the more Luther discovered that the sinner was justified by the mercy of God through faith alone, the more he could hear the psalmist's own voice without having to resort to what could be called a "typological move" that made all the Psalms speak with Jesus' voice. To be sure, Christ too prayed the Psalms—one thinks particularly of Psalm 22—but he prayed not simply for humanity as Savior but with humanity as a fellow believer. Thus, what moved Luther's interpretation of the Psalms was not the movement from the Old Testament shadow to the New Testament reality but rather the faith-creating promise of God.

This was why Luther could write in 1521 that the Hebrew Scriptures were the swaddling clothes in which the Christ Child was wrapped.[28] As will become clear in chapter 3, however, calling Scripture the manger or swaddling bands actually provided a very different approach to Scripture, one that relied on the foolishness of Scripture when compared to reason. "We must be prepared to search and find the Child in the manger (that is, in Scripture) so that we hang on tightly to the Word. Otherwise there are simply fleeting thoughts from hearsay that do not remain firm."[29] Already in his prefatory remarks to the Christmas gospel (John 1:1–14) in his *Church Postil*, Luther gave precedence to the Old Testament. "Thus, they [the apostolic writers] base all of their preaching on the Old Testament, and there is no word in the New Testament for which an Old Testament word does not stand behind it, where it was proclaimed beforehand. . . . For the New Testament is nothing other than a revelation of the Old Testament, just as when someone first had a sealed letter and then broke it open."[30]

By 1528, this approach—hearing believers' cries to God in the Psalms—came to full expression in Luther's preface to his translation of the Psalter. He now found true faith in God at the center of this remarkable book of the Bible. Thus, he could write:

A human heart is like a ship on a wild sea, driven by the storm winds from the four corners of the world. Here it is struck with fear and worry about impending disaster; there comes grief and sadness because of

28. WA 10/1/1:15, 4–5 (=LW 35:122).
29. WA 17/2:312, 17–20.
30. WA 10/1/1:181, 24–182, 1 (=LW 52:41).

present evil. Here breathes a breeze of hope and of anticipated happiness; there blows security and joy in present blessings. These storm winds teach us to speak with earnestness, to open the heart and pour out what lies at the bottom of it. He who is stuck in fear and need speaks of misfortune quite differently from him who floats on joy; and he who floats on joy speaks and sings of joy quite differently from him who is stuck in fear. When a sad man laughs or a glad man weeps, they say, he does not do so from the heart; that is, the depths of the heart are not open, and what is in them does not come out.

What is the greatest thing in the Psalter but this earnest speaking amid these storm winds of every kind? Where does one find finer words of joy than in the psalms of praise and thanksgiving? There you look into the hearts of all the saints, as into fair and pleasant gardens, yes, as into heaven itself. There you see what fine and pleasant flowers of the heart spring up from all sorts of fair and happy thoughts toward God, because of his blessings. On the other hand, where do you find deeper, more sorrowful, more pitiful words of sadness than in the psalms of lamentation? There again you look into the hearts of all the saints, as into death, yes, as into hell itself. How gloomy and dark it is there, with all kinds of troubled forebodings about the wrath of God! So too, when they speak of fear and hope, they use such words that no painter could so depict for you fear or hope, and no Cicero or other orator so portray them.

And that they speak these words to God and with God, this, I repeat, is the best thing of all. This gives the words double earnestness and life. For when people speak with others about these matters, what they say does not come so powerfully from the heart; it does not burn and live, is not so urgent. Hence it is that the Psalter is the book of all saints; and everyone, in whatever situation they may be, finds in that situation psalms and words that fit their case, that suit them, as if they were put there just for their sake, so that they could not put it better themselves, or find or wish for anything better.[31]

For Luther, the entire Old Testament was filled with believers and sinners, with commands and promises, with terror and comfort. In this way, it is simply filled to overflowing with Christ, the Savior of the

---

31. The translation by Charles M. Jacobs (revised by E. Theodore Bachmann) found in LW 35:255–56, which uses the original preface as published in 1528 (WA DB 10/1:100, 33–38 and 102, 1–27).

world, because it is filled with believers clinging to God's promises. Thus, because the Hebrew Scriptures profess faith in the true God, they too fall under Luther's dictum "*Was Christum treibet.*"

Sola Scriptura?

Finally, one of the most surprising things about Luther's view of authority has to do with the famous phrase *sola Scriptura*.[32] There are three famous *solas*—*sola Scriptura*, *sola gratia*, and *sola fide* (Scripture alone, grace alone, by faith alone)—often used among English-speaking Lutherans and other Protestants since at least the nineteenth century to summarize Luther's thought. Using the critical Weimar edition of Luther's works online and its search engine, one can now determine how often Luther used these phrases in all their permutations in his Latin works.[33] The results? *Sola gratia*: two hundred times; *sola fide*: twelve hundred times; *sola Scriptura*: twenty times. Twenty times! Moreover, a closer look at those twenty occurrences leads to even more surprises. Two are references not to Luther's writings but to his opponents'. Both Cardinal Cajetan in 1518 and Erasmus of Rotterdam in 1524 offered to debate Luther (more or less) on the basis of *sola Scriptura*, using Scripture alone. So that leaves just eighteen cases.

Of these remaining occurrences, some actually undercut the notion that Scripture was the *only* authority for Luther. One of the most striking came in his famous "Proposition Thirteen." When in 1519 John Eck proposed twelve theses for his debate in Leipzig with Luther (he had composed others for his debate with Karlstadt), Luther countered by publishing a thirteenth proposition on papal authority, to which he offered a lengthy defense. After a thorough discussion of biblical texts, he stated, "So that it would not appear that I am discussing Scripture alone," and went on to recount other authorities that supported his position.[34] Here Luther actually *refused* to approach the

---

32. This section of this chapter has been published in a slightly different form as "A Note on 'Sola Scriptura' in Martin Luther's Writings," *Luther-Bulletin* 20 (2011): 21–31.

33. In his German writings, Luther also used some equivalent phrases. For this study, however, it is enough to note his use (or lack thereof) of the now-famous Latin terms.

34. WA 2:227, 30–31.

question of papal authority *de iure divino* (by divine right), which was the theme of his proposition, with Scripture alone!

In 1522, Martin Luther's attack on Henry VIII and that king's tract defending the seven sacraments included another peculiar reference to *sola Scriptura*. Here Luther distinguished extrabiblical doctrines from biblical ones. He provided a list (papacy, conciliar decrees, teachers, indulgences, purgatory, the [sacrifice of the] Mass, the universities, monastic vows, episcopal idols, human traditions, cult of the saints, and new sacraments) of things that Satan had secretly sown in the church through his chief idol, the pope. The papacy in particular had completely departed from Scripture. Luther then reflected on his own life under the papacy, when "I was content to expurgate the Scriptures alone [*solas Scripturas*]" for the sake of papal authority, until Christ showed Luther's spirit a different path.[35] Luther described his position under papacy as "anything but Scripture."

One of the most sophisticated rejections of *sola Scriptura* by Luther came in his 1522 preface to Philip Melanchthon's annotations on Romans and 1 and 2 Corinthians. By publishing these lecture notes on Scripture, which Luther had purloined from Melanchthon, Luther seemed to be undermining any call to read Scripture alone.[36] After praising these annotations, which included the first rhetorical analysis of Paul's letter to the Romans, Luther then posed Melanchthon's obvious objection to their publication. "You say, 'Scripture alone must be read without commentaries.' You say this correctly about the commentaries of Origen, Jerome, and Thomas [Aquinas]. They wrote commentaries in which they handed down their own ideas rather than Pauline or Christian ones. Let no one call your annotations a commentary but only an index for reading Scripture and knowing Christ."[37] Luther had no place in his vocabulary for a reading of Scripture that excluded commentary. On the contrary, there was a place for indexes to Scripture (that is, something more than Scripture alone) precisely because they did not hand down the author's own ideas but only Scripture and Christ. Later, in his Genesis commentary

---

35. WA 10/2:186, 40–187, 1.
36. See Timothy J. Wengert, *Philip Melanchthon's* Annotationes in Johannem *in Relation to Its Predecessors and Contemporaries* (Geneva: Librairie Droz, 1987), 33.
37. WA 10/2:310, 12–16.

he stated, "For this reason I hate my books, and I often want to bury them because I fear lest the readers stay with them and abandon the reading of Scripture, which alone is the font of all wisdom."[38] Note that he did not say Scripture was the only wisdom but, using that familiar humanist metaphor, the font of it.

Luther also recognized the dangers of claiming to construct doctrine on the basis of Scripture alone. In a preface to his lectures on Jonah from 1526, appropriately dedicated to his colleague Justus Jonas, Luther took aim at those who "promise all things for themselves by the sole reading of the Scriptures, and that so presumptuously."[39] The *sola lectio Scripturarum* was no compliment in Luther's mind because, as he had already warned Jonas, these people (papists and perhaps especially Erasmus) could not separate Scripture's teaching about justification by faith without works from their own distorted views. Another example of the same skepticism came in Luther's lectures on 1 John in 1526–27. Again, the context made clear that he was not eliminating other authorities but actually discussing how to appropriate such authorities into the interpretation of Scripture. He began with the remark that "it is very rare that there are pure teachers in the church. Only Scripture is pure."[40] Luther did not, however, exclude other authorities, as if he were saying that Scripture alone were authoritative. The purity of Scripture had specifically to do with justification by faith as opposed to monastic vows—that is, "*Was Christum treibet!*"

Luther faced the same problem in a sermon on Matthew 7 for the eighth Sunday after Trinity in 1528. He had to deal with the problem of false prophets and the common axiom that Scripture was the book of heretics. Despite such sayings, he insisted that "Scripture alone must remain."[41] His point? Despite a variety of interpretations of Scripture, one was not to let Scripture go but instead notice what kind of interpreter was speaking and what the fruits of his or her teaching were. Jesus warned his disciples about wolves *in sheep's clothing*—that is,

38. WA 43:93, 40–94, 3 (=LW 3:305–6).

39. WA 19:177.

40. WA 20:745, 2–3 (from the copy of the lecture by Georg Rörer, not used by LW 30:295).

41. WA 27:287, 6.

wolves who claimed legitimate authority (like the papists). Evil might begin by using Scripture, but it would always end badly. The bad fruits spoken of in this text, he continued, were not simply murder or adultery but the mortal sin of the "most beautiful, subtle lies." Here again Luther's push to figure out the fruit of scriptural interpretation pointed his listeners toward distinguishing law and gospel so that they asked whether the teaching brought the consolation of faith or simply more works. Perhaps one could paraphrase Luther as holding to a principle of *sola Scriptura et fructus eius* (Scripture alone and its fruits). Thus for Luther *sola Scriptura* did not eliminate the use of other authorities in this world except with respect to Scripture's own provenance: justification by faith alone.

To be sure, there are places where Luther supported a view of "Scripture alone." However, in each of these cases, he used the phrase not abstractly, as if it were a hard and fast principle, but always in relation to something else. It was Scripture alone, and not the papacy, not monasticism, not works righteousness, Luther opined. Thus the very criterion Luther used for putting James in an appendix he also used with respect to biblical authority. It was always a matter of Scripture *and its fruits*. Moreover, "Scripture alone" was actually a christological principle. It was Scripture alone precisely because this book alone pushed Christ. Thus, once again, the very principles of interpretation and authority at work in Luther's sophisticated judgment of James bore fruit in his use of the phrase *sola Scriptura*. Indeed, we would be better off replacing *sola Scriptura* with the phrase *solus Christus* (Christ alone) and, what amounts to the same thing, *solo Verbo*, by the Word alone—where "the Word" was for Luther not simply the Bible but its proclamation.[42] Thus, already in 1522 Luther could write about the church that it is not a "quill house" but a "mouth house."[43] God's Word was God's Word when proclaimed "for you," not when shut up in a book, where it was good only for others or for nothing.

---

42. Willem Jan Kooiman, *Luther and the Bible*, trans. John Schmidt (Philadelphia: Muhlenberg, 1961), 42: "*Sola scriptura* (scripture alone) is the same as *solus Christus* (Christ alone), and that is again the same as *sola gratia* (grace alone) and *sola fide* (faith alone)."

43. WA 10/1/2:48, 5, cited in Eric W. Gritsch, *Martin—God's Court Jester: Luther in Retrospect* (Philadelphia: Fortress, 1983), 98.

Luther's 1520 *Assertion of All Articles* (against the papal bull of excommunication), after pointing out the deficiencies in the church fathers, stated, "I do not wish to be considered more learned than all [of them], but I wish for Scripture alone to reign. Nor do I wish it to be interpreted by my spirit or that of any other human beings, but I wish it to be understood through itself and by its own spirit."[44] That this was hardly a plea for using "Scripture alone" in some sort of reductionistic manner was proved by Luther's next sentence, where to justify and authorize his own position he referred to Augustine's appeal to Scripture. Moreover, Luther's point was not even simply allowing one passage in Scripture to interpret another but to allow Scripture to be its own interpreter in terms of its chief point ("through itself and by its own spirit"). "By its own spirit" refers again to the self-authenticating Scripture—that is, with what the law and gospel do to people (namely, make them believers, as we will see in chapter 2).

Another sermon also demonstrates admirably how Luther connected faith and Scripture. Preaching on 1 Corinthians 15 on the first Wednesday after Easter in 1529, Luther commented on the phrase, "according to the Scripture" (1 Cor. 15:3). Reason did not understand that "in this stinking body is placed a new life like the sun." One listener reverted to Latin in his notes, stating: "To remain in Scripture alone nourishes faith."[45] Here again Luther did not offer a principle for constructing theologically true statements but instead appealed to nourishing faith: "*Was Christum treibet.*"

Two conversations preserved in the *Table Talk* sum up Luther's view of Scripture and its authority. In 1533, Luther looked back at his life and talked about what he was going to leave to posterity.

44. WA 7:98, 40–99, 2. In his book on Luther and the Council, Christopher Spehr (*Luther und das Konzil* [Tübingen: Mohr Siebeck, 2010], 261) misconstrues Luther's argument in the *Assertio omnium articulorum* and assumes that the Reformer had narrowed his view of authority to Scripture, when in fact the very passage he cites (WA 7:100, 12–14) proves the opposite—namely, that Scripture and the witness of the church fathers have authority, just not at the same level: "Nevertheless, through this argument [about Scripture] I do not want to take away authority from the Fathers and to repay with ingratitude for their holy labors but to place higher the freedom of the Spirit and the majesty of the Word of God."

45. WA 29:331, 15–17 (cf. Martin Luther, *The 1529 Holy Week and Easter Sermons of Dr. Martin Luther*, trans. Irving L. Sandberg [St. Louis: Concordia, 1999], 175).

> If God wants to take me away this very hour or tomorrow, this is what I will leave behind: that I want to acknowledge Christ as my Lord, and I do this not only out of Scripture but also out of experience, because the name of Christ has often helped me where no one else was able to help. So I have on my behalf the substance and the words—that is, experience and Scripture—and God has given both to me in very large measure. But it has been really bitter for me through assaults—but that has also been good for me.[46]

Scripture *and* the experience of faith combine to make Luther a biblical theologian. Luther also claims that his enemies would never be able to withstand the kinds of assaults he has endured.

The second example, this time from 1538, reveals one of the few moments where Wittenberg theologians directly discussed the question of *sola Scriptura*. Justus Jonas remarked that "Scripture contains such wisdom that one is unable to learn it thoroughly." Luther replied, "We really have to remain students of the Holy Scripture."[47] He went on to defy his companions to interpret 1 Peter 4:13 ("Rejoice in tribulations") and criticized people whom he called Epicureans and arrogant know-it-alls who were done with Scripture after one reading.

Thus, Scripture alone, read without faith and the experience of the cross, results not in coming to the truth but in leading the weak astray. Only when Scripture is approached as the inexhaustible resource that it truly is—as God's Word that kills and makes alive (2 Cor. 3:6) and thus as something that will not succumb to our categories, principles, or proof texting—will it drive us away from itself and toward faith in Christ under the cross. Would that this more lively view of Scripture would replace our shibboleths, old and new, with a living encounter with our Lord Christ!

---

46. WA TR 1:240 (no. 518) (=LW 54:94).
47. WA TR 4:27 (no. 3946).

2

Method

Dying and Rising

L uther and his followers developed a unique method for interpreting Scripture. It is so different, so alien, from any of the
methods in current use among American Christians that his
immediate descendants sometimes seem embarrassed to talk about
it. What this chapter will demonstrate is just how other methods
of interpreting Scripture always risk turning good news into bad,
and then it will trace the development of Luther's own approach to
Scripture that carefully distinguished law and gospel.

A Cautionary Tale about Throwing Stones

To illustrate just how revolutionary this approach is, consider how
we may interpret the story of the woman taken in adultery. In trying
to judge sexual ethics today, a person might say, "It's not that our
church should not forgive such people, but we have to follow Jesus'
example in John 8 and tell them, 'Go, and sin no more.' What do you
say to that?" What *does* one say to that? Is this the way to proceed

with this verse? Find a sinner, lift their condemnation, and tell them not to do it again? What does one say?

In fact, this interpretation is not new and stands in a very long line of biblical interpreters of that text and others. And, although we often do not realize this, the method employed to interpret this biblical text can *only* result in moralizing and, taken to an extreme, legalism. That is, it is a method of interpretation that is dominated by the law—but in such a way so that the law applies to others and not so much to the individual doing the interpreting. The rules for this method are simple and seductive. First, Jesus becomes a model for us to follow. "WWJD" are four of the most destructive letters in the English theological alphabet when it comes to interpreting the Bible. "What would Jesus do?" ensures that whatever we find in Scripture describing Jesus (or any saint, for that matter), even the most gracious of actions, simply becomes a "must." Jesus died? We must die for others. Jesus multiplied loaves? We must share with others. Jesus warned a woman? We must warn others. Jesus was merciful? We must be merciful. When Jesus becomes an example, we are once again stuck with those Latin gerunds described in the last chapter: what *must* be believed, done, and hoped for (*credenda*, *agenda*, and *speranda*).

Already in the earliest phases of the Reformation, both Martin Luther and Philip Melanchthon insisted—*insisted*—that (in their words) we do not simply turn Jesus into another Moses—that is, a lawgiver.[1] Of course Jesus is an *exemplum*, an example. The entire Western Christian tradition, beginning with Augustine, who coined the phrase, had said as much. But far more important—in fact central, as Luther had already argued in *The Freedom of a Christian*—was the other thing that Augustine had emphasized: Jesus was also *sacramentum* (that is, saving gift from God). WWJD? He would hit you over the head and say, "Get over it! Stop turning me into a lawgiver! It is not about you and your precious rules and how you clobber others with them; it is about the grace and mercy of God." In fact, in this

---

1. See Luther's introduction to his very first German commentary on the appointed Sunday texts for the Christmas season, the *Weihnachtspostil*, titled "A Brief Instruction, What One Should Search for and Expect in the Gospels" (WA 10/1/1:10, 20–14, 15 [=LW 35:113–24]).

very story of the woman taken in adultery, that *is* what he does. We just cannot believe it, cannot hear it.

So the pervasive legalistic interpretation of this story always implies that it is about following Jesus' example. But, second, this approach also always deflects judgment from the interpreter and turns the law loose on others. That is the favorite pastime of the elder brother in Jesus' parable in Luke, who cannot imagine why his father would be so gracious to such a renegade and why he never let him roast his 4-H calf with his friends, to steal a line from the *Cotton Patch Gospel*. This is what we easily do regarding the story from John 8. Consider this. This story, which is not found in the earliest manuscripts of John and sometimes shows up in Luke, has three statements from Jesus— apart from his writing in the sand, whatever that means. First, Jesus issues a word of permission to those who would judge the woman. Then he speaks a declaration to the woman. Finally, he issues her an invitation. So WDJD? What *did* Jesus do? Simple: permission, declaration, and invitation.

It is easy to ignore Jesus' first word in this text. In fact, it is the one word that we can and should easily generalize to include not only the crowd of Palestinian men eager to stone the poor woman but also *anyone* who would judge anyone else. "Let the one without sin cast the first stone." There. All human beings have permission from the very Son of God to judge others. There is, however, one small caveat: be without sin. "Hmmm! Well, maybe not today. I'll come back to-morrow; I think I just heard my mother calling." And so the crowd melts away. What happened? Jesus preached the law, and it worked. Preaching the law is not a matter of making people feel guilty; it is not a matter of condemning others; it is not even simply a matter of using imperatives rather than indicatives in speech. Instead, preaching the law is simply a matter of telling the truth about the human situa-tion. Or, to employ a useful metaphor from Alcoholics Anonymous, preaching the law mentions the elephant in the room—that is to say, mentions the unmentionable. And here? The unmentionable is hypoc-risy, a desperate cover-up of our own sin by declaring someone else to be a sinner. So, with a word of permission, "Let the one without sin throw the first stone," suddenly the crowd melts away. The law, which allowed the stoning of adulterers and adulteresses and which these concerned citizens wanted to use on others, Jesus simply used on the accusers in the form of a permission slip. "Are you without sin? Fire away!" And that is the word in the story that applies to all of us. When one insists on using the phrase "Go, and sin no more" against those in same-gendered, committed relationships as another stone to throw, permission is granted to throw—*if* we have no sin.

Of course, here human beings, perhaps especially preachers, get worried. "Can't we preach the law at all? What about all of those kinky things that I am sure are going on in my congregation?" "Ah," to use Luther's words, "now do you smell the roast?" The law is being preached in this text, and Jesus is not getting rid of it, but it is being preached against the accusers, not against others—not against open sinners caught *in flagrante delicto*. The human creature's skill at getting out from under the law is breathtaking. We most worry about saving the integrity of the law for others when the law actually condemns us. After all, what bigger law is there than the one against being judgmental? The law against judging others goes back to the garden of Eden and that original temptation: "You will be like gods, deciding what is right and wrong" (Gen. 3:5).[2]

At the heart of our legalism lurks our breaking of the first commandment, our idolatry of self. In this story from John, this is where the problem truly lies. Some interpreters, who (like the rest of us) probably are eager to avoid judging themselves, imagine that Jesus simply was writing the commandments in the sand and that the bystanders would see the one they had broken and then leave. Perhaps, but then he only had to write down one: "You shall have no other gods." "First, take the beam out of your own eye." "Judge not." The woman broke the sixth commandment; her accusers, by taking judgment into their

2. The literal phrase in Hebrew, "knowing good and evil," occurs three times in the Bible. In addition to its use in Gen. 3, we hear Barzillai in 2 Sam. 19:35 asking David to allow him to retire (in the literal translation of the King James Version), "I am this day fourscore years old: and can I discern between good and evil?" Then, in Isa. 7:15–16, the child prophesied by Isaiah will not have reached the age of decision (as we call it)—that is, "before the child knows how to refuse the evil and choose the good" (NRSV)—before the kingdoms threatening Judah will be deserted. Thus, it is not so much about *knowing* good and evil but taking charge and deciding what's right and what's wrong. We should perhaps call this tree in Eden the "I-can-decide-for-myself-what's-right-and-what's-wrong tree."

own hands, broke the first. And that, more than anything else, is what the law reveals and condemns.

Jesus' other two words, of declaration and invitation, reveal a third problem in the way this story gets used. Legalism always makes it impossible to apply God's promises to the neighbor and always forces a confusion of law and gospel. "Is no one here to condemn you?" Jesus begins with a question but only to set up one of the most remarkable paradoxes in all of Scripture: "Neither do I condemn you." "But wait, Jesus," the judging sinner objects. "I mean, you have no sin." Even if this story about Jesus was smuggled into the text by some later writer, it now sits between John the Baptist's declaration ("Behold, the lamb of God," John 1:29, 36) and the Gospel writer's own testimony: "Not a bone in this spotless lamb" (19:36), sacrificed at the very moment that Passover lambs were being sacrificed in the Temple, "not a bone shall be broken." So here he is, the one and only one who could throw the first stone, *and he does not do it*. What is going on here?

Once we realize how absurd it is for Jesus *not* to condemn, then we can hear, finally hear, how great the gap is between Jesus' question ("Is no one left to condemn you?") and his declaration ("Neither do I condemn you"). And that gap is filled by the cross itself. The "neither do I condemn you" is the same as the forgiveness of the man dropped through the roof in Mark 2, the forgiveness of Peter's denial in John 21, the forgiveness from the cross for his torturers in Luke 23. And his lifting of the condemnation is of a completely different nature from the crowd's behavior: skulking away muttering about their sins while dropping stones meant for the kill. What Jesus does in that moment, simply put, is end the law. End it completely, because here it is no longer just a matter of temporarily giving the woman a stay of execution ("Let the one without sin take the first toss") and keeping the law in place. No, the law is now ended. The one and only one who could condemn, who could cast the first stone, does not do it! St. Paul—who understood this story completely even if he never heard it—wrote, "Now, therefore, there is no more condemnation for those who are in Christ Jesus" (Rom. 8:1). *Mirabile dictu!* This woman is in Christ Jesus, and so is every sinner within the sound of his voice, so that, therefore, there is no condemnation for her or for us, judgmental sinners though we are. The gospel on Jesus' lips simply tells the truth about God, who is filled with mercy and grace alone.

Only in that light can Jesus' final word be understood. Disconnect his invitation from his declaration, his ending of the law with its condemnation from his call to live, and everything will always only be distorted and drive hearers to one form of legalistic excess or another. Either we will revel in sinning or we will use the invitation as a club to beat others into the ground. What is impossible to imagine—to believe!—is that Jesus invites human sinners to live without condemnation. When we want to join in throwing stones at and condemning others, all that remains for us is condemnation for ourselves and others. This invitation, "Go, and sin no more," is not spoken to us when we have rocks in our hands to throw at others; it is only spoken to us when our accusers have left the building and we are kneeling helpless and alone before the Savior of the world—and are filled with faith by the power of his declaration: "Neither do I condemn." Then it is an invitation to *us*, not a further condemnation for us to use on others.

Jesus speaks this word of invitation to us: "Go, and sin no more!" When that becomes clear, what happens? The very first thing that happens is that the invitation slips out of our hands, and we hear only law. Consider the following experiment: Jesus says to you right now, "Go, and sin no more!" So, how are you doing? "Huh?" the judging sinner answers. Since, say, Sunday when you may last have heard the absolution, how have you been doing?[3] "Uh-oh." Do you feel dragged out by your hair, out of your favorite sin, and into the middle of the public square? Surrounded by people ready to throw rocks?

---

3. It is a tradition in Lutheran churches in this country to begin each worship service with the confession of sins and absolution. Of course, some congregations never hear the pastor utter an unconditional word of forgiveness ("You are forgiven"). Either they frame it as a subjunctive ("May God forgive" or "God forgive you"), which may or may not apply to the sinner, or (again in imitation of churches where there is only condemnation and law) the confession and forgiveness are simply omitted completely, replaced by exhortations to lead better lives. For the centrality of the "Sacrament of Absolution," as the early Lutherans called it, see Timothy J. Wengert, *A Formula for Parish Practice: Using the Formula of Concord in the Parish* (Grand Rapids: Eerdmans, 2006), 16–46.

If all it takes is "How are you doing?" to destroy the invitation, what happens after the invitation melts away? Here is where the experiment gets personal. "Go, and sin no more!" So, how is it going? "Well," one could say, "I haven't been doing very well lately, but give me a little more time, and I'll try a little harder, and. . ." It is amazing how quickly this invitation, when applied to oneself, becomes a treadmill or, rather, a millstone. But—and here's the astounding thing about this story—when the invitation turns back into condemnation, then it is driving us back to the One in whom there is no condemnation.

But what if someone said, "Well, I've been doing pretty well, especially if you compare me to . . ."? Then the invitation dissipates in a different way by becoming an excuse to accuse others all over again. Then the "Go, and sin no more" is no longer invitation for us but condemnation for others, and then we are back among the accusers, to whom Jesus gives permission to judge if we are without sin. But, of course, to judge another is the greatest sin of all because it makes us into gods, deciding good and evil.

Well, then, how does this invitation stay or become a real invitation? To continue with the experiment: Jesus says right now, "Neither do I condemn you. Go, and sin no more." That is, you do not *have* to sin any longer. If the law and its condemnation are not lifted, you have to sin; but now, in Christ, there is no more condemnation. "Well," one might respond, "you cannot run a country this way!" That is true; but Jesus is not about shoring up constitutions and penal codes (more on the first use of the law below) but about something far different. He is about the new world coming in the water of baptism, in bread and wine, and in words—and on the cross, where the law with its condemnation comes to a final end, where God sets aside "the record that stood against us with its legal demands . . . nailing it to the cross" (Col. 2:14). In that new world, as we live on the edge of it, there is no condemnation. So go ahead—go, and sin no more.

It is a risky thing, announcing this word of unconditional forgiveness, of an end to the law and an invitation to live. What if people believed it? Of course, if people do not believe that sins can be declared forgiven, it will be the death of preachers everywhere! If pastors thought they were in trouble in the parish before, let them try announcing the unconditional forgiveness of sins. See where that gets them. It got Jesus accused of blasphemy and finally killed (see Mark 2:1–12).

What if, having heard this declaration and invitation, someone goes out and sins again? It could happen. What does one do then? Well, that depends. If one's brother or sister sins against someone personally, it means that one can forgive them up to 490 times a day per sin. But what if the sin is against others, against God? Of course, pastors are in the business of forgiving other people their sins against God. After all, Jesus says, "Whoever hears you, hears me" (Luke 10:16). So, whatever the pastor forgives on earth shall be forgiven in heaven, to borrow a phrase from John 20:23. There would seem to be no limit to announcing God's forgiveness to the sinner, but it must be at least 490 times per sin per day as a safe bet, and it includes forgiving the sin of judging others. When Jesus said, "Go, and sin no more," he did not say to the believing brother or sister, "Go, and forgive no more."

Distinguishing Law and Gospel

Luther's method of scriptural interpretation is simple: the proper dividing of Scripture—that is, the distinguishing of law and gospel. This is at the heart of the matter. Luther employed the terms in publications at least from 1519 and on through until his death. We find the distinction in Philip Melanchthon already in his 1521 theological textbook, the *Loci communes theologici* ("common theological topics"), and throughout the rest of his life as well. Indeed, Melanchthon did not write commentary on any book of the Bible without making this distinction in the introduction. The woodcut that graced later editions of the complete Luther Bible throughout Luther's lifetime distinguished law and gospel, so as to inform readers visually, before they had read a single word, what method they should use to understand Scripture. But Wittenberg's earliest Reformers weren't the only ones who used this distinction. Law and gospel were also important for second-generation Lutheran theologians such as Martin Chemnitz, Joachim Mörlin, Matthias Flacius, and even Georg Major. It is the central concept from the Reformation that distinguished these early Lutheran biblical interpreters from all the other exegetes of the period. It also continued to be central to later Lutherans, including, in the

United States, C. F. W. Walther, Robert Bertram, and Gerhard Forde, and in Germany, Werner Elert, Oswald Bayer, and Gerhard Ebeling, among many other examples.[4]

To understand how the distinction between law and gospel functions, one must realize that there are three ways to define law and gospel, where only the third one gets to the heart of this method. First, people use law and gospel simply to distinguish commands from promises. While it is true that Scripture is full of imperatives and indicatives, this misses the mark. Thus, if a person reads a text that includes a command and says, "Oh, that must be law," he or she has not yet said anything very important.

Second, and this comes from some things that Luther himself said as he tried to find simple ways to explain the distinction, sometimes law and gospel are defined as differentiating the books of the Old Testament (law) from the New Testament (gospel). As Kenneth Hagen indicates in his research on Luther's interpretation of Hebrews, this only really works for Luther if one does not capitalize "old" and "new."[5] That is, it only works in the realization that these words do not have to do with specific books of the Bible and whether they were written before or after Christ. Instead, as will be clear below, the terms *law* and *gospel* have to do with God's Word spoken for the old creature (law) or for the new (gospel).[6]

So, what did the distinction between law and gospel *really* mean for the Reformers? Here we come to the third way to define law and gospel, which grants us access to a central insight of Luther's Reformation. Understanding the Bible as Word of God does not have to do

4. C. F. W. Walther, *The Proper Distinction between Law and Gospel: Thirty-Nine Evening Lectures*, trans. W. H. T. Dau (St. Louis: Concordia, 1929); Robert W. Bertram, *A Time for Confessing*, ed. Michael Hoy (Grand Rapids: Eerdmans, 2008); Gerhard Forde, *Theology Is for Proclamation* (Minneapolis: Fortress, 1990); Werner Elert, *The Structure of Lutheranism*, 2nd ed., trans. Walter A. Hansen (St. Louis: Concordia, 1962); Oswald Bayer, *Theology the Lutheran Way*, ed. and trans. Jeffrey G. Silcock and Mark Mattes (Grand Rapids: Eerdmans, 2007); Gerhard Ebeling, *Luther: An Introduction to His Thought*, trans. R. A. Wilson (Philadelphia: Fortress, 1970).

5. Kenneth Hagen, *A Theology of Testament in the Young Luther: The Lectures on Hebrews* (Leiden: Brill, 1974).

6. Heinrich Bornkamm deals with this confusing terminology in *Luther and the Old Testament*, trans. Eric W. and Ruth C. Gritsch (Philadelphia: Fortress, 1969), 81–87.

so much with what a text is or means or with its relative position in the canon of Scripture as with what it *does* to its hearers. When the Reformers used the words *law* and *gospel*, they were actually observing how God's Word works on hearers or, even better, how God uses commands and promises on us.[7]

Turning first to the law, the Reformers came to realize that God uses it in two distinct ways. The first, or civil use of the law, has to do with how God uses the law to maintain order and restrain evil (see below). It is a use connected to this world and God's good creation. It is bound to the world of judges, justice and jail, stop signs and traffic tickets. The second, or theological use, which is the chief use of the law as far as these early Lutherans were concerned, has to do with how God uses the law to reveal sin; to terrify the comfortable, self-satisfied person; and to put to death the old creature. As Paul writes in 2 Corinthians 3:6, "the letter kills"; or in Romans 3:20, "by the law comes knowledge of sin"; or in Galatians 2:19, "I through the law died to the law."

In the light of this second, theological use of the law, God's use of the gospel on hearers is a perfect match. God uses the gospel to end the law and its accusation: the law reveals sin, and the gospel forgives it; the law terrifies the comfortable, and the gospel comforts the terrified; the law puts to death, and the gospel makes alive. Thus, Philip Melanchthon wrote about this distinction in article 12 of the Apology (Defense) of the Augsburg Confession:

> For these are the two chief works of God in human beings: to terrify and to justify the terrified or make them alive. The entire Scripture is divided into these two works. One part is the law, which reveals, denounces, and condemns sin. The second part is the gospel—that is, the promise of grace given in Christ. This promise is constantly repeated throughout the entire Scripture: first it was given to Adam, later to the patriarchs, then illuminated by the prophets, and finally proclaimed and offered by Christ among the Jews, and spread throughout the entire world by the apostles. For all the saints have been justified by

7. See Gerhard Forde, *Where God Meets Man: Luther's Down-to-Earth Approach to the Gospel* (Minneapolis: Augsburg, 1972), 7–17; and Wengert, *Formula for Parish Practice*, 77–89.

faith in this promise and not on account of their own sorrow for sin out of fear of God or love of God.[8]

What does this mean for the interpretation of Scripture? First, it means this: if people only read Scripture to find out what it meant or what it means, it will always and only be the dead, killing letter. It will never make anyone alive, least of all those reading or hearing it. In this connection, Luther distinguished theologically between a noun (*Heisselwort*; literally, a word that labels) and a verb (*Thettelwort*; literally, an action word). All that human words can do is label something. But God never simply labels things with God's Word; God does something to us by killing and making alive—that is, by destroying all of the idols with which we prop up our lives and by making us new.[9] After all, when God says, "Let there be light," there is light. God's Word works on us.

Second, it means that Lutheran Pietism's way of construing these terms (an approach, incidentally, that all American Lutherans have inherited from their immediate forebears) distorts this concept terribly and in two ways.[10] First, Pietism, like later forms of evangelicalism, often assumed that the preacher was in charge of doing what only God does—namely, killing and making alive. This meant that the burden was on the preacher to bring forth the proper Christian "affections," as they called them. This led immediately to a second distortion: law and gospel were understood as first making people feel guilty (law) and then remedying their guilt (gospel). On the contrary, sinners do not need to *feel* guilty. They need, rather, to hear that they *are* guilty—however that may make them feel. This means that, for the preacher or the biblical interpreter, distinguishing law and

8. Ap XII.53, in BC, 195.
9. See Luther's *Confession concerning Christ's Supper*, WA 26:282–85 (=LW 37:180–84).
10. Pietism, a movement in Lutheranism similar to certain forms of Puritanism and Methodism within Reformed and Anglican circles, often stressed conversion, sanctification, and Christian good works over faith, forgiveness, and the sacraments. It traces its beginnings in Germany to Philip Jakob Spener, pastor in Frankfurt, Germany, and his publication in 1675 of *Pia desideria*, a preface to sermons by Johannes Arndt. For more on this important movement in later Lutheranism, see Carter Lindberg, ed., *The Pietist Theologians: An Introduction to Theology in the Seventeenth and Eighteenth Centuries* (Oxford: Blackwell, 2005).

gospel is simply a matter of telling, one after the other, two truths: the truth about the human condition (law) and the truth about God in Christ (gospel).

One can observe how the law was preached in the Bible itself. Nathan says to David (2 Sam. 12:7), after telling him a sweet story about the poor person with one little lamb whose lamb is stolen by the rich man with massive flocks, "You are the man!" And David responds (v. 13), "I have sinned." In Acts 2, Peter simply states: "This Jesus, whom you crucified, God has raised." And the text goes on to say that they were cut to the heart. Jesus simply tells the rich man in Mark 10:21, "One thing you lack!" and the man is stricken. Of course, these simple "truths" about the human condition, because they mention the unmentionable, work on the hearers and strip them bare, reveal sin, terrify, and (using Paul's language) put to death.

The gospel, then, is simply a matter of telling the truth about God, a truth that the Holy Spirit uses to forgive and make alive. Peter's audience is driven to cry out, "What then can we do?" His answer is baptism for the forgiveness of sins—not something they *do* at all but what God does through the means of grace. When Jesus' disciples, hearing how hard it will be for the rich to enter heaven, cry, "Who then can be saved?" he answers, "With mortals it is impossible, but not with God; with God nothing is impossible!" (Mark 10:26–27). Or, in the story of the man dropped through the roof (Mark 2:1–12), Jesus just says, "Your sins are forgiven." Of course, Pharisees and pious folk of all kinds cannot stand it and grumble in the back of the room—for them, the gospel acts as law. But for the man, Jesus shows in healing his body what has happened in the man's heart. Indeed, all of the miracle stories are simply pictures of gospel and resurrection. The gospel makes believers out of unbelievers—which is the same as raising the dead. This, then, is the heart of a distinctly "Lutheran" interpretation of the Bible: distinguishing law and gospel and thus telling the truth about the human condition and about God.

There is one caveat to the preaching of the law. One must first make sure that the biblical text applies. In the mid-1520s, one teaching that Luther had to confront came from, among others, Andreas Bodenstein von Karlstadt, who argued that Christians in his day needed to observe certain Old Testament commandments, especially tithing and

Sabbath-keeping. Luther's response made clear that he employed a radically different approach to reading Scripture. He wrote,

> One must deal cleanly with the Scriptures. From the very beginning the Word has come to us in various ways. It is not enough simply to look and see whether this is God's Word, whether God has spoken it; rather we must look and see to whom it has been spoken, whether it fits us. That makes all the difference between night and day. . . . The Word in Scripture is of two kinds: the first does not pertain or apply to me, the other kind does. . . . The false prophets pitch in and say, "Dear people, this is the Word of God." This is true; we cannot deny it. But we are not that "people."[11]

Yes, the Bible says it. But does it apply in this situation to these people? This too is an important part of hearing the commands and promises of Scripture.

The Law's First Use: The Pastor as Vo-Tech Teacher

Something needs saying about the first use of the law—that is, the civil use. Many people have also neglected this aspect of Luther's insight into Scripture. This civil use of the law is, of course, more at home in city hall than in the pulpit, but it is surprising how easy it is to miss the opportunity to talk about texts that tell the truth about the human need for order and the restraint of evil in this life—order that matches the beauty of creation and the intent of the Creator (revealed only to the eyes of faith) and restraint that shows how, even in a flawed and fallen world, God still loves the creation.

Although this is not the law's chief function, nevertheless there are remarkable passages in Scripture that show how people ought to behave in this life toward their neighbors. To be sure, Luther did not think that Scripture was the only place to find good moral teaching. Indeed, over the centuries Christians have used all kinds of extrabiblical sources: Aristotle, Plato, Cicero, Buddha, John Stuart Mill, Will

11. LW 35:170, with minor corrections (WA 16:384, 19; 385, 7–16). I am grateful to Vitor Westhelle's use of this text in *The Church Event: Call and Challenge of a Church Protestant* (Minneapolis: Fortress, 2010), 66, for making me once again aware of it.

Rogers—you name it, Christians may use it. The reason for Luther's openness goes back to the notion that God has two hands. With the right hand, God uses law (second use) and gospel to make believers. With the left hand, however, God rules in this world quite apart from the gospel: keeping order and restraining evil.[12] Because of sin, this rule is often distorted and imperfect. Nevertheless, God has written basic standards of moral behavior on everyone's hearts, so that we do not first have to make the world Christian before we can establish justice and peace. In fact, one of the fastest routes to injustice and conflict is to insist on Christian supremacy in such matters and thus confuse God's two hands.

Christians do have one advantage over non-Christians when it comes to works in the world, but it arises exactly where it should: not in the doing of good things but in faith itself. Perhaps Philip Melanchthon's most successful foray into this issue came in his 1528 commentary on Colossians. In a fifty-page excursus on God's two-handed righteousness (civil righteousness for this world; Christ's righteousness in forgiveness for the breaking in of the new world), he asked the question of what advantage Christians had in this world. Answer? Christians trust that the things they do on earth are God's callings. Melanchthon realized, for example, that there was a divine calling not simply to be a ruler but also to be a subject.[13] A year later Martin Luther reflected similarly in the Large Catechism that God established not only the offices of parent, householder, employer, teacher, pastor, and magistrate but also the offices of child, servant, employee, student, congregant, and citizen.[14]

When we boast of a biblical or Christian morality, we are often looking for some special ethic that applies only to Christians, what both Luther and Melanchthon, borrowing a line from Colossians

---

12. See, for example, Gustav Wingren, *Luther on Vocation*, trans. Carl C. Rasmussen (Philadelphia: Muhlenberg, 1957), and Paul Althaus, *The Ethics of Martin Luther*, trans. Robert C. Schultz (Philadelphia: Fortress, 1972), for broader discussions of this topic, as well as D. Michael Bennethum, *Listen! God Is Calling: Luther Speaks of Vocation, Faith, and Work* (Minneapolis: Augsburg Fortress, 2003).

13. See Timothy J. Wengert, *Human Freedom, Christian Righteousness: Philip Melanchthon's Exegetical Dispute with Erasmus of Rotterdam* (New York: Oxford University Press, 1998), 123–36.

14. LC, Ten Commandments, 103–78, in BC, 400–410.

2:23, labeled "self-chosen spirituality." In their day, it was monasticism, which was touted as providing a second baptism and a way to
perform meritorious super works. Today, it may be the "purpose-driven
life," retreats in rural Washington State, special trips to third-world
countries, or inflexible stands on abortion, firearms, capital punishment, and all the rest. Or perhaps it is just a matter of no drinking,
no smoking, and no dancing. Against this, the Reformers insisted that
in the Bible daily life *is* the Christian life. This is the life of changing
diapers, hauling manure, and paying taxes. It is rarely talked about
in the New Testament simply because it is assumed.

Yet Luther's creative, insightful way of reading Scripture revealed
all kinds of small hints of this daily life. Romans 13:1–7 (NRSV) actually commends paying "taxes to whom taxes are due," and Romans
13:8–10 insists that we love our neighbor as ourselves. Ephesians 4:28
suggests that the thief stop stealing and get a decent job. But Luther
saw this notion in other places too. The shepherds, instead of making
a pilgrimage or building a monastery, simply returned to their flocks,
Luke says (2:20).[15] For Luther and his hearers, this was a revelation.
Believers could tend sheep; they did not need to join a monastery or
go on a pilgrimage. One of his most lyrical expositions of this down-
to-earth faith that daily life *is* the Christian life came from the Large
Catechism in comments on the fourth commandment.

> If this could be impressed on the poor people, a servant girl would
> dance for joy and praise and thank God; and with her careful work,
> for which she receives sustenance and wages, she would obtain a trea-
> sure such as those who are regarded as the greatest saints do not have.
> Is it not a tremendous honor to know this and to say, "If you do your
> daily household chores, that is better than the holiness and austere
> life of all the monks"? Moreover, you have the promise [included in
> this commandment] that whatever you do will prosper and fare well.
> How could you be more blessed or lead a holier life, as far as works
> are concerned? In God's sight it is actually faith that makes a person
> holy; it alone serves God, while our works serve people. Here you have
> every blessing, protection, and shelter under the Lord, and, what is

15. See *The Martin Luther Christmas Book*, comp. Roland H. Bainton (Philadelphia:
Muhlenberg, 1948); cf. WA 10/1/1:137, 14–138, 12 and WA 37:246, 11–248, 26.

more, a joyful conscience and a gracious God who will reward you a hundredfold. You are a true nobleman if you are simply upright and obedient.[16]

A Third Use for the Law: The First and the Second Uses Apply to Believers

We need to say a few words about the notorious "third use" of the law, a disputed category in Lutheran thought since the 1550s.[17] We will define the term below, but first of all it is necessary to understand how the category arose. In 1520, Luther and Melanchthon simply talked about the gospel and what is now labeled the "second use" of the law. Had a good Lutheran candidacy committee interviewed them about their fitness to become pastors in 1520 and asked about a civil or "first" use of the law, neither would have passed muster, because they had not yet "invented" such a category. In 1521, Luther was in hiding in the Wartburg Castle, working on his *Christmas Postil*, the commentary on the Sunday pericope texts for the Christmas season (the same one-year cycle from the medieval church that many Lutherans used up until 1978). He got to New Year's Day (Gal. 3:23–29) and was reading (or at least recalling) Nicholas of Lyra's commentary on this text, where Nicholas (the medieval exegete who produced a commentary on the entire Bible) wrote that the Jews had four ways to use the law. Luther passed over two uses without mention and then universalized the other two, putting them in God's hands: in the first place, he wrote, God used the law to restrain evil and maintain order, and, in the second place, God used the law theologically to show sin and drive people to Christ and the gospel.[18]

16. LC, Ten Commandments, 145–48, in BC, 406–7.

17. Reformed theologians, beginning with John Calvin, also discussed three uses of the law, where what the Lutherans call the third use was understood to be its central use. See John Calvin, *Institutes of the Christian Religion*, ed. John T. McNeill, trans. Ford Lewis Battles, 2 vols. (Philadelphia: Westminster, 1960), 1:360 (*Institutes* II.vii.12): "The third and principal use, which pertains more closely to the proper purpose of the law, finds its place among believers in whose hearts the Spirit of God already lives and reigns."

18. WA 10/1/1:449–503, especially 458–63, commenting on Gal. 3:23 and the "fruits" of the law. Luther's *Postil* for the entire church year was translated into English

Melanchthon, who saw Luther's *Postil* through the presses, then began to employ this distinction in his writings, counting two uses right up through 1532, when he published a third commentary on Romans.[19] In 1534, however, when revising his commentary on Colossians for a third time, right where he had defined two uses of the law in 1527 and 1528, Melanchthon added a third use. Luther, whose theology revolved around the death of the old and birth of the new, on the one hand, and around the two hands of God, on the other, never had recourse to this third use. Why did Melanchthon add it? First, he wanted to make clear that Lutherans were not licentious or antinomian. He had already had fights in the late 1520s with John Agricola, Luther's student (and later the chief antinomian Lutheran), so he knew the danger firsthand. On top of that, in 1534 Melanchthon also was engaged in conversations with moderate Roman Catholics, meeting in Leipzig. They insisted that, based upon John 13:34 ("that you love one another . . . as I have loved you"), the term *gospel* had to include the law. Melanchthon, in order to make it clear that such commands were not gospel and to prevent the gospel from becoming law, insisted that even commands given to Christians were still law and not gospel, which he defined as the free forgiveness of sins of the gospel. Thus, for Melanchthon, the "third use" of the law simply described commands given to believers (and hence not to be confused with the gospel's promises)—commands that helped them determine which works were good and pleasing to God.

Unfortunately for Melanchthon's distinctions, a young theologian by the name of John Calvin read Melanchthon's work and took the

---

at the turn of the last century. See Martin Luther, *Sermons of Martin Luther*, ed. and trans. John Nicholas Lenker, 8 vols. (Minneapolis: Luther Press, 1905–8; repr., Grand Rapids: Baker, 1989), 6:267–310, especially 270–72 (here, 271–72): "Here, indeed, is evident the necessity for the Law, and the purpose it serves—God's design in it—its office being twofold: First to preserve discipline among us; to impel us to an honorable outward life. . . . Second, God's design in the Law is to enable man to know himself; to perceive the false and unjustified state of his heart; to discover how far he is from God and how utterly impotent his own nature is . . . to be humbled in consequence of such knowledge and come to the cross, yearning for Christ, longing for his grace, despairing of himself and placing all his hope in Christ."

19. For this paragraph, see Timothy J. Wengert, *Law and Gospel: Philip Melanchthon's Debate with John Agricola of Eisleben over Poenitentia* (Grand Rapids: Baker, 1997), 177–210.

concept into his own theology, except that he made the third use the chief use and defined it as the special guide for Christians, which included laws not revealed to other human beings.[20] Usually, when Lutherans now demand a third use of the law, what they want is Calvin's approach. For Melanchthon and later Lutherans, however, the third use of the law was simply the first and second use applied to Christians.[21] Believers are at the same time saint and sinner, believer and unbeliever, and thus they still need the law—first, to restrain them and reveal God's good and gracious will and order for humanity and for all of God's creation and, second, to kill the old creature and drive it back to the gospel, faith, and God-pleasing works and away from works-righteousness and "self-chosen spirituality."

But there is another question that may be asked in this regard, and that is, "When is the law not the law?" Sometimes the law is not a condemning command but rather enticing invitation. Take the second commandment, "You shall not take the name of the Lord your God in vain." This command restrains evil by condemning false witness using God's name, and it maintains order by putting God's name in a special place. It shows us our sin and condemns the old creature, both when we use God's name for nothing more than a punctuation mark in our sentences and also, far worse, when preachers and other leaders in the church teach and preach all manner of legalistic foolishness under the cover of God's name. The number of preachers who stand condemned by this commandment every time they end their sermons with the law and rob people of the comfort of the gospel is staggering.[22]

But what if God's name is more like the case of a young teen's first girlfriend, who has an unlisted phone number? And, all of a sudden, sitting there in class, she comes swishing down the row of desks in a flurry of skirts and perfume designed to make an eighth-grade boy's head spin. And there on his desk appears a small slip of paper, with (as was common in the 1960s) two letters and five numbers on one

20. See Calvin, *Institutes of the Christian Religion*, II.vii.12.
21. See Wengert, *Formula for Parish Practice*, 90–102.
22. See LC, Ten Commandments, 54, in BC, 393: "The greatest abuse [of God's name], however, is in spiritual matters, which affect the conscience, when false preachers arise and present their lying nonsense as God's Word."

side and a command on the other: "Call me!" Now, it is a command, to be sure, but not to the young fellow in love, who uses every opportunity to fulfill that command, yet without ever imagining that he is doing a "good work" or "earning" her favor. Nor would he dream of scrawling her number on a bathroom wall ("For a good time, call Margie"). Never! Suddenly, a command becomes an invitation, an enticement. Inasmuch as the boy is in love, nothing is a burden; nothing a duty; nothing drudgery. Instead, it is completely free. Just so, as Luther reminded readers of the Small Catechism, the reason God gives us his name is so that "instead we may call on him in every need: by praying, praising, and giving thanks."[23] It is an invitation to come to our heavenly Father as dear children come to their dear father, as Luther then explained the introduction to the Lord's Prayer.[24]

Years later, discussing the third use of the law, the sixth article of the Formula of Concord, a Lutheran statement of unity published in 1580 long after Luther and Melanchthon had died, put it this way:

> However, when people are born again through the Spirit of God and set free from the law (that is, liberated from its driving powers and driven by the Spirit of Christ), they live according to the unchanging will of God, as comprehended in the law, and do everything, insofar as they are reborn, from a free and merry spirit.[25]

What better way to describe the Christian life than to speak of a "free and merry spirit." When thinking about this free and merry spirit, perhaps one could imagine Opie in the closing moments of the old *Andy Griffith Show*, fishing pole in hand, holding his father's hand and walking down a wooded path, whistling. That is the free and merry spirit, doing spontaneously and freely, *by faith alone*, everything that God invites it to do. Or one could imagine the command on that love note, which gives the law a whole new meaning. So unless people come out of church whistling, the preacher is probably not preaching the law in terms of this third use at all but instead is simply burdening souls with one more thing to do to get right with God.

23. SC, Ten Commandments, 4, in BC, 352.
24. SC, Lord's Prayer, 2, in BC, 356.
25. Formula of Concord, Solid Declaration, VI, 17, in BC, 590.

Exegesis Is for Proclamation: Finding the Law and the Gospel in the Text

How, in addition to the extended example that began this chapter, can we observe these distinctions working within actual biblical texts? Starting with the last point (the third use of the law), take, for example, Jesus' line in John 16:23: "Ask the Father for anything in my name, and he will give it to you." This has to be one of the most abused texts in all of Scripture. We have televangelists on the one side, using this passage to bribe people into imagining that material wealth is the heart of the Christian message and leaving people completely devastated when they do not get what they need or want. On another side, we have similar groups who turn this little promise into a big command. "You've gotta ask, and if you don't, God will never give you anything. Moreover, if you don't get what you've asked for, it means you don't have enough faith." The law and its judgment loom large in both approaches. Of course, many preachers, embarrassed to death by this unconditional promise, try a third way by making up excuses for why God does not answer our prayers, without going to the extreme of blaming the hearers for not praying hard or earnestly enough or for not having enough faith.

What is the problem with all of these approaches? No faith! Or, more accurately, no relation to God! That is, the interpreters view God either as a celestial Santa, a nasty lawgiver, or a stingy giver. In any case, it seems as if it is up to the reader or hearer either to make this text work or to get John's Jesus off the hook for saying such silly things. But faith (that is, true relation to God based on trust in God's promises and assurance that God is God and we are not), which Gerhard Forde defined as falling in love,[26] hears a different word altogether.

A preacher on this text once put it this way.[27] Suppose you and your spouse love to dance, and you are on the dance floor in her arms, and she looks at you and says, "I love you. Ask me anything, and I'll do it." Of course, you could abuse her invitation and pretend that it is all about you and satisfying your basest desires. ("You'll do anything?

26. Forde, *Where God Meets Man*, 65–67.
27. The sermon of Irving L. Sandberg, delivered in the 1980s and sent to me at that time.

How about letting me commit adultery?") But you are in the arms of your lover, and you are gliding across the room, doing what you love the most, and you are in love. So, what else could you possibly ask for except for another dance, and another, and another? In just this same way, when Jesus says, "Ask anything," there is only one answer that the believer, the faith-filled lover, can give: "I just want you!" Indeed, that is exactly what had happened eight chapters earlier in John 6:67–69. "You my disciples, will you also leave?" Jesus asks. And a wide-eyed Peter responds for all believers everywhere, "Lord, to whom shall we go? You have the words of eternal life, and we have believed and have known that you are the Holy One of God." No wonder that the standard "Alleluia Verse" in some Lutheran hymnals since 1978 has used these words for the congregation to sing before reading the gospel.

To be sure, the command to "ask anything" forces us to pray (as in the first use of the law). Of course, it reveals our lack of faith in God's promises and our failure to pray (as in the second use of the law). But deep inside these words, when read with the eyes and ears of faith, one hears God's heartbeat and the voice of the beloved, and we fall in love all over again and simply ask for another turn around the dance floor. "Ask anything!" And faith responds, "Amen! Come, Lord Jesus!" What else is there?

So much for the third use of the law. With the second use of the law, the biggest problem that preachers and teachers face is their own old creature. The Bible is remarkably clear; the readers and preachers are the ones who are often in a fog. They simply cannot believe their ears or eyes when they read the Bible. After all, if they did, it would kill them! Consider two examples from the Gospels of Matthew and Mark.

Take Jesus' statements about divorce in Matthew 19:9. "Whoever divorces his wife . . . and marries another commits adultery against her; and if she divorces her husband and marries another, she commits adultery." Every three years this text comes up in the series of appointed Sunday texts that many churches now use.[28] Every time it is read,

28. The notion that preachers should choose their own texts, championed by some scholars, is foolish and dangerous. There is enough in the appointed readings to last even the best preacher at least nine years (twelve, if one preaches on the Psalms too),

everyone gets very, very quiet. Why? In twenty-first-century American culture, everyone knows divorced and remarried Christians—many are themselves divorced and remarried—and this text bothers everybody. Now, if the words of Jesus cause such silence after two thousand years, we know that they have the power to kill, to reveal our sin. But what exactly does that mean? Does the text simply reveal the sins of others whom, if only we were as strict as in the good old days, we would prevent from being a part of the Christian community? (That, in some ways, is to this day the answer of the Roman Catholic Church, with its demands for annulments.) Once again we have rocks in our hands, ready to throw at others.

Instead, the text reveals *our* sin, the sin of all of us. We live in a world where marriages fail, where the God-given goal of the union between a man and a woman gets destroyed in all manner of ways, and where one spouse can and does abandon the other. In our country, a remarkable percentage of the chronically poor and homeless are divorced or abandoned women and their children. And that kind of abandonment is no less sinful than adultery, especially where divorce is simply another way to practice serial polygamy. We are, *all of us*, stuck in and complicit in a world that does not work. In the words of the cartoon character Pogo, "We have met the enemy, and he is us." The Matthew text, when properly read, taught, and preached, should send all of us running pell-mell to the Savior, begging forgiveness and blessing, which is just what Mark does by following the statement on divorce with the blessing of the children and of all other weak and abandoned ones.

How, then, should one preach on it? By telling the truth! We live and are part of just such a broken, fallen world. For some married folk, this text may reveal their own complicity in the death of a relationship; but others may simply be killing one another with thoughts and words while remaining married, while the rest of us resent paying

---

and the danger of destroying the ecumenical spirit in which the current readings were devised (answering the reservation Luther had about coming up with his own set of readings in the sixteenth century) and of taking the congregation captive to the preacher's own whims is enormous. After all, a professor at a Lutheran seminary *may* know what texts to choose, but what are the chances that every pastor will as well? Instead of helping people read the Bible, it may actually prevent it.

taxes to support the poor and needy divorced women and their children. Worse yet, when the blessing of the gospel, Jesus' blessing, is offered to these poor folk, it is religious folk (such as the disciples) who get in the way. But Jesus sits there surrounded by women and children—the most vulnerable in his society and ours—and gives them a word, or rather, *the* Word: "Do not get in their way; this is what God's kingdom is made of" (Mark 10:13–16). And then, using his hands in those days (but employing the waters of baptism in our day), he blesses them.

Another example of God's second use of the law comes with the words, "If any would be my disciples, let them deny themselves, take up their cross and follow me" (Mark 8:34). What usually happens when preachers read this text is simply this: we cannot take it the way it actually sounds, so we deny the text rather than deny ourselves. In fact, if the truth be told, we cannot—absolutely cannot—take this text literally, because it is meant to kill us, to crucify us. Here we again need to pay attention to the context: Peter's confession of faith in Jesus as Messiah and his immediate denial of Jesus' crucifixion. It is followed by a miracle story in which the father of the boy with an unclean spirit, when faced with the call to faith, answers the way Peter behaved: "Lord, I believe; help my unbelief!" (Mark 9:24). When it comes to this text, all of us are believing unbelievers, Christ-confessing and cross-denying. This text does not give us something *to do*; this text *does* something to us.

Consider how this text kills us when taken literally. "Let them deny themselves." "OK, I am going to try. I, Timothy John Wengert, hereby officially deny myself." There is, however, something wrong with this attempt. I cannot do it, and the reason is simply this: the "I," the self, is still the subject of the sentence. The very thing *I* want to deny, *I* cannot. No one can do it. And if we preach or teach self-denial, it will never, ever work. No one can do it, even if preachers yell at the top of their lungs. What usually happens, of course, is that the preacher tones down the demand and pretends the text does not say what it says. "Deny yourself" comes to mean "give up whale meat for Lent" (something my sister and I were good at while we were growing up) or "put more in the offering plate" or some such thing. The same is true for "take up your cross." We always prefer the balsa wood versions that don't really put us out, or we rail against the idea that crosses are placed on us without our say-so, despite the fact that, as Luther wrote, "Even as we live each day, death our life embraces."[29] Or, as Paul put it, "We are sheep for the slaughter" (Rom. 8:36).

Well, why would Jesus give an impossible command? They are *all* impossible. All of them! It is just that "denying ourselves" is the most impossible of all. Its very impossibility finally does to us what we cannot do to ourselves: it denies us and crucifies us with the plain facts—the truth of the human situation—that we cannot deny ourselves, cannot bear the cross, cannot follow Christ any more than Peter could. It finally puts us where Jesus wanted to put Peter in the first place: behind him, following after him, dying to self, an unbelieving believer. How does one preach the law here? By simply reading the text and asking oneself and one's congregation this simple question: How are you doing? The Word will do the rest.

This brings us to the gospel: telling the truth about God. Of course, the good news (what God has done, is doing, and will do) is all over the Bible. The trouble is that preachers, readers, and listeners always come, literally, with an *agenda*—that Latin gerund for "things that must be done" by us. The gospel, however, is not about us. Instead, it always and only puts God as the subject of the theological sentence. God acts. God suffers and dies. God raises Jesus from the dead. Jesus heals, forgives, blesses, and all the rest. So, when reading or listening to the Bible, one hears all that God does, and, when it comes time to preach and teach, one simply lets the gospel out of the bag and surrounds it with baptism, absolution, and the Lord's Supper (just in case the preacher goofs up that week). After all, the best illustration of the gospel in any sermon is simply to point to the font and the table—that is, to point to the crucified and risen Savior, who comes in water and the Word and in bread and wine and the Word.

Small wonder that the artist Lucas Cranach depicted Martin Luther on the Wittenberg altarpiece, completed in 1547 shortly after Luther's death, in two different poses. Underneath the main picture of the Last Supper, Luther is simply standing in Wittenberg's pulpit, pointing,

---

29. See LW 53:274–76 and *The Lutheran Book of Worship* (Minneapolis: The American Lutheran Church, 1978), no. 350.

like John the Baptist, to Christ on the cross, the Lamb of God who takes away the sin of the world. And in the Last Supper scene itself, Luther is seated among the apostles, depicted as he only looked in 1521 (wearing a beard), and turning to give a sixteenth-century layperson the chalice—something that the church had forbidden since 1215 and that first happened at that very altar in 1521. Cranach caught the heart of the Lutheran method for biblical interpretation and for worship: pointing to Christ and distributing his body and blood— that is, dying and rising with the Savior. That depiction sums up the preacher's task and the heart of the gospel: Christ crucified and risen for us and our salvation!

3

Interpretation

Strength Perfected in Weakness

That person is worthy to be called a theologian who understands the visible things and the backside of God viewed through sufferings and the cross. A theologian of glory calls evil good and good evil. A theologian of the cross calls a thing what it is."[1] With these words from the 1518 Heidelberg Disputation, Martin Luther introduced his theology of the cross. What the New Testament professor Erik Heen has recently shown is that one can rigorously apply the theology of the cross to the interpretation of Scripture.[2] That is the goal for this chapter.

Before we can use the theology of the cross in this way, however, we need to define it properly. Many people, on first hearing the phrase, immediately assume that the theology of the cross was simply Luther's theory about why Jesus died. It was not. Instead, the theology of the cross was for him the *"revelatio Dei sub contrario specie"*—that is, the revelation of God under the appearance of the opposite—God in

---

1. WA 1:354, 19–22 (=LW 31:40).

2. Erik Heen, "The Theological Interpretation of the Bible," *Lutheran Quarterly* 21 (2007): 373–403.

the last place you or I would reasonably look.[3] This is the way Luther put it in *The Bondage of the Will*, his attack on Erasmus of Rotterdam:

> Faith has to do with things that do not appear [Hebrews 11:1]. There-fore, in order that there may be a place for faith, it is necessary that all things that are believed are hidden. Not that they are hidden by being more remote but rather *under the opposite object, sense, and experience*. Thus, when God makes alive, he does it by killing; when he justifies, he does it by making guilty; when he transports into heaven he does it by leading down into hell, as the Scripture says, "The Lord kills and makes alive, he leads into hell and back up again" (1 Sam. 2[:6]). . . . Thus God hides clemency and mercy under eternal wrath, righteousness under iniquity. . . . Otherwise there would be no need for faith.[4]

Luther said much the same thing in his explanations to the Heidelberg theses. Notice how law and gospel, justification by faith and this revelation of God hidden in suffering, combine.

> Opposed to the invisible things are the backside and visible things of God—that is, the humanity, the weakness, the foolish things, as 1 Cor. 1:25 calls the weakness and foolishness of God. For, since human beings have abused the knowledge of God derived from works, God wanted instead to be known from sufferings and to reprove that wisdom of invisible things through the wisdom of visible things, so that those who did not worship the God manifest from works might worship the God hidden in suffering. As 1 Cor. 1:21 says, "Because in the wisdom of God the world did not know God through wisdom, it pleased God through the foolishness of preaching to save those who believe. . . ." Thus, in John 14:8, when Philip said, according to a theology of glory, "Show us the Father," Jesus immediately called him back and refocused his transitory thought of seeking God elsewhere on Jesus himself, saying,

---

3. Luther did not use this phrase exactly, but it accurately sums up his point. See Walter von Loewenich, *Luther's Theology of the Cross*, trans. Herbert J. A. Bouman (Minneapolis: Augsburg, 1976); Gerhard Forde, *On Being a Theologian of the Cross: Reflections on Luther's Heidelberg Disputation, 1518* (Grand Rapids: Eerdmans, 1997); Timothy J. Wengert, "'Peace, Peace . . . Cross, Cross': Reflections on How Martin Luther Relates the Theology of the Cross to Suffering," *Theology Today* 59 (2002): 190–205.

4. WA 18:633, 7–21 (=LW 33:62), emphasis added.

"Philip, who sees me, sees my Father." Therefore in Christ crucified is true theology and knowledge. And in John 10, "No one comes to the Father except through me. I am the gate, etc."[5]

God is revealed "hidden . . . under the opposite object, sense, or experience," God in the brokenness of the cross, the emptiness of unbelief, the guilt of sin. There is here no glory of miracles or of almighty power. Here there is only the foolishness of what we preach. What Erik Heen has shown is that this theology of the cross is not simply revealed in Scripture—it is the heart of Scripture itself. We worship a foolish, weak God revealed in a foolish, weak book. The central mistake people make when approaching Scripture is to think that this revelation should somehow be qualitatively different from the crucified God it reveals, but it is not.

Paul demonstrates this in 1 Corinthians 1–2. He begins by stating that his proclamation itself is weak and foolish. Of course, fully thirteen books in the New Testament are ascribed to this chief of sinners, so, at the very least, thirteen of twenty-seven books are weak. In fact, however, weakness is precisely what makes the New Testament inspired, God-breathed. For Paul does not stop with just calling his message weak. Instead, he looks at his listeners and discovers that they too are weak: "Consider your own call, brothers and sisters: not many of you were wise by human standards, not many were powerful. . . . But God chose what is foolish in the world to shame the wise; God chose what is weak in the world to shame the strong; God chose what is low and despised in the world, things that are not, to reduce to nothing things that are, so that no one might boast in the presence of God" (1 Cor. 1:26–29 NRSV). Finally, Paul even looks at himself and in chapter 2 reminds his readers, "When I came to you, brothers and sisters, I did not come proclaiming the mystery of God to you in lofty words or wisdom. For I decided to know nothing among you except Jesus Christ, and him crucified. And I came to you in weakness and in fear and in much trembling" (vv. 1–3 NRSV). Then, at the end of 2 Corinthians (12:9 NRSV, alternate reading), Paul reveals this scandalous oracle of God: "My grace is sufficient for you; my power is

5. WA 1:362, 4–19 (=LW 31:52–53).

made perfect in weakness." So, in Paul we have a weak message from a weak speaker to weak hearers. And *that* describes the entire Bible.

The Weakness of Scripture

Why is it so hard to believe this same weakness regarding Scripture itself, when according to Paul it is in the message, the hearers, and the apostolic messenger? We have already touched on this problem in chapter 1. Here, all we need to do is look at the text from 2 Timothy 3:16: "All Scripture is given by inspiration of God—God-breathed—and is profitable." Whereas modern American religiosity has often fixated on securing the first half of this sentence and, in some instances, insisted on an inerrant and infallible book, Luther and the Reformers were interested in the last three words: "and is profitable." If we insist on the wisdom and strength of the Bible—measured, of course, by human standards—then it will not profit us one wit. That is, it will never fulfill its purpose of doing God to us but will leave us to lord it over Scripture with our reasonable explanations and thirst for power.

In contrast, as soon as we hear Scripture under the cross and in its weakness and foolishness, it reveals God's true power and wisdom by killing and making alive, as we saw in chapter 2. In the hands of the Holy Spirit, Scripture becomes—in its very weakness!—the idol-destroying, faith-creating Word of God, reducing hearer, proclaimer, and proclamation to weakness and foolishness, just as Paul insists. And it does this in two ways.

First, Scripture itself is externally foolish. It is written in dead languages, and all the people by whom and to whom it was written are dead. It is filled with stories about foolish, weak people—losers one and all: refugees named Sarah and Abraham; a crooked fellow named Jacob; wandering escapees from Egypt; stammering Moses, sinning Aaron and Miriam; adulterous David; cranky prophets; doubting Thomas, denying Peter, betraying Judas, and a crucified Messiah. Moreover, from our perspective, the Bible's social realities are also preeminently unwise and impotent. These people are as trapped in their patriarchal, vengeful age as we are in ours, and no amount of exegetical sleight of hand is going to rescue them or us.

Second, Scripture is also internally foolish; that is, it is filled with *believers*, people who trust God—and the God they trust is crucified! Reasonably speaking, God makes one mistake after another in this book: promises an offspring to Abraham and Sarah, so the first thing Abraham does is try to pass Sarah off as his sister; lets Jacob, the evil twin brother, get the blessing; chooses Moses and that ragtag band of slaves instead of powerful Pharaoh and his army; keeps adulterous David on the throne (to say nothing of Solomon); can find no one better than a dresser of sycamore trees, Amos, to announce the word of judgment to Israel. And then there is all of this stuff involving a manger, a man standing soaking wet in the Jordan next to an oddly dressed baptizer, and a crucified criminal who at his resurrection chooses to appear to women, to fishermen, and, "as to one untimely born" (1 Cor. 15:8), to a persecutor of the church, Paul! Yet through all of this, there are believers, people who trust this God despite punishment, abandonment, unanswered prayers, suffering, death, and all the rest.

For the most part, Philip Melanchthon, Luther's right-hand man in Wittenberg, did not generally appreciate the oppositions inherent in the theology of the cross. He did not consider paradox a legitimate theological category and treated it instead as a rhetorical one. But in one respect, Melanchthon embraced this notion and developed what could be called an ecclesiology of the cross.[6] In the face of the powerful claims by his papal opponents to apostolic succession, greater numbers, and a bigger army, Melanchthon pointed to the weak first-century church, which included Mary and Joseph, Elizabeth and Zechariah, and the shepherds. Their witness was not a powerful word but a weak one, filled with cultural and social weaknesses, to be sure, but also pointing to weak believers in the crucified Christ. So, for Melanchthon and Luther, the church itself was hidden in weakness, visible only in its marks of Word, sacraments, and suffering.

The same weakness both Luther and Melanchthon celebrated in the church is also true for Scripture. It is a weak book from all external and internal signs, proclaiming a weak God coming in the dust—visibly hidden in weakness. And that very weakness is its strength, for that

6. Timothy J. Wengert, "Caspar Cruciger Sr.'s 1546 'Enarratio' on John's Gospel: An Experiment in Ecclesiological Exegesis," *Church History* 61 (1992): 60–74.

is the way God comes to us in this book: humble and lowly, riding into Jerusalem on a donkey, not with lofty words of wisdom but in weakness and trembling.

If Scripture is so weak and foolish—and it is—why do American Christians today have such trouble believing, teaching, and preaching its weakness and foolishness? Part of the answer lies in the social situation. Americans live in the most powerful nation on earth with one of the highest per capita incomes. They seek a powerful God to match their own claims to power, and a powerful Scripture as well. This lust for power spills over into definitions of church, so that American Christians often worship the kingdom, power, and glory there too. Just look at what passes for church, as the airways and bookstalls fairly groan with the powerful messages of a host of televangelists and megachurch pastors. And this message finds eager listeners around the world precisely for the same reason that American consumer-isms of other kinds are so successful. What becomes of Americans' purpose-driven lives or abundant lives when the planet is wrapped in a self-induced heat wave or a selfishly induced economic meltdown? What is the point of living if all flesh is grass? As long as American preachers avoid telling the truth about the human condition in this context, their hearers will be stuck looking for a strong, wise Bible.

But the problem runs even deeper than this, because our thirst for a strong Bible goes back to the garden of Eden. Luther discovered in Eve's encounter with the snake all human tendencies regarding God's Word. To the snake's "Did God say . . . ?" Eve should really have answered, "I don't know; go ask God." But instead, she entered into conversation with the snake, and in her attempt to defend God already violated the first commandment by setting up her own reason as God.[7] It is there that our lust for a powerful word began. It was then exacerbated when God finally caught up with the couple in the garden: "The woman, *whom you gave me*," the man began, and al-ready one sees the heart of the old creature's power-filled theological argumentation. "The snake, *whom you made*," the woman continued. That is to say, human beings were so desperate to have the last word that they used God's Word (God did give the woman and create the

7. See WA 42:116–17 (=LW 1:155).

snake—it is in the Bible) against God. A powerful Word of God is the old creature's last, desperate attempt to stay alive and to avoid God's living Word of judgment: "Dying you shall surely die" (Gen. 2:17). As punishment for such Bible-thumping, work is cursed; childbearing is cursed; snakes are cursed. There is nothing but struggle, which finally breaks out into the open in chapter 4, where the first believer, Abel, was slain by the first unbeliever, Cain, thus setting up the struggle between the old and the new that will continue until Christ comes again.[8]

But the struggle also takes place over the electing Word of God. Abel I loved; Cain I hated. Jacob I loved; Esau I hated. God is forever choosing the weak, the despised, the neglected—including especially a weak, despised, and neglected book, written by losers for losers—from Abel to Paul and beyond. The scandal of God speaking through the pages of the Bible is as great as the scandal of the crucified God who hangs on a cross and comes in bread and wine. This scandal, by the way, relates to Luther's criticism of James described in the first chapter. To put it in the terms of this chapter: the problem with James is that it is too strong. It pushes the law—God's law, to be sure, but law nevertheless. Yet apostles—and pastors and preachers are all apostles—have only one office, to bear witness to Christ crucified and risen again for the life of the world. That is all anyone has: God's weakness in Christ *is* the believer's strength. This is not what the world wants, not what the old creature wants, not what "the Old Evil Foe" wants, and so they conspire to get believers to turn this book into power and wisdom—the more infallible and inerrant the better. Yet at every turn the book itself opposes them with a God who chooses Abraham and Sarah, rescues Israel, brings a remnant back from Babylon, and raises the Crucified from the dead.

Finding the Central Weakness of Scripture: Romans

Interpreters of the Bible who follow the lead of Luther and Melanchthon are often charged with having a "canon within the canon"—that

---

8. This is the heart of Philip Melanchthon's understanding of world history and especially the history of the church. See Timothy J. Wengert, "Philip Melanchthon on Time and History in the Reformation," *Consensus* 30, no. 2 (2005): 9–33.

is, a smaller set of texts or books within the canon of Scripture that they then favor over others, interpreting everything through this narrower lens. Surely this is a foolish thing to do to such a disparate collection of rules, oracles, and stories. While it is easy to become defensive and point out that such Lutherans interpret the entire Bible, in the end these interpreters of the Bible ought really to own up to it. Lutherans really do have a canon within the canon, and they can be proud of the weakness of such an approach. What no one remembers is where this canon within a canon came from or why it is so important.

From the way this flaw is often described, it would seem that these interpreters simply played an old pious trick with the Bible: cut it open to a random page and decided that would be the center. That is, Luther arbitrarily chose Paul and justification and law and gospel. He could have just as easily chosen something else. Indeed, sophisticates of all kinds like to say something like this: "You Lutherans start with Romans, but we start with John" or Matthew or some other book.

Of course, this is hardly what happened. Luther started lecturing on the Psalms and, if we can trust the description of his breakthrough written down by Luther's pastor, Johannes Bugenhagen, and recently discovered by Martin Lohrmann, it is the *Psalter*'s use of the righteousness of God that bothered him, not Paul's.[9] Moreover, it was Augustine in *On the Trinity* who first put Luther on to a Pauline interpretation of the phrase that rescued him from the condemnation of the law. Then Luther turned to Paul (lecturing on Romans, Galatians, and Hebrews from 1515 to 1518) and to Augustine's *On the Spirit and the Letter* (which he used in his interpretation of Romans), only to emerge in 1519 to tackle the Psalter all over again, after having discovered, as mentioned in chapter 1, the faithful synagogue—believers in God.

Not only is the beginning of the story about the Lutheristic canon within a canon distorted, so that Luther and later Lutherans end up diagnosed with an obsessive-compulsive Pauline disorder, but the later parts of the story are twisted as well. Luther, who never published a commentary on Romans (as opposed to two on Galatians), is now being accused of not even getting Romans right and messing up

9. Martin Lohrmann, "A Newly Discovered Report of Luther's Reformation Breakthrough from Johannes Bugenhagen's 1550 Jonah Commentary," *Lutheran Quarterly* 22 (2008): 324–29.

justification. Philip Melanchthon, who published five separate commentaries on Romans, is almost entirely neglected by modern biblical scholars, echoing in practice the opinion of an early eighteenth-century publisher of a "nonpartisan" history of the church who accused Melanchthon of abandoning Scripture altogether in favor of philosophy.[10] Not only did Lutherans have a canon within the canon of Scripture, but also, according to the "New Perspective on Paul," their canon was not even in the canon.[11]

Here a little history can help. First, Luther and Melanchthon were both rightfully humanists. That is, like the scholars of their age, they used the very latest biblical methods. The humanist's cry was "*bonae litterae*," use good Latin and read good books, and "*ad fontes*," get back to the purest sources. No wonder that the next generations of Lutherans, when describing the Bible in the Formula of Concord, did not call it inerrant or infallible but "the pure, clear fountain of Israel." Now, one of the things that distinguished the humanist or Renaissance reading of Scripture from that of their scholastic predecessors was their understanding that the books of the Bible were actually books, written by real authors with real hearers and real methods of communicating. Thus, for example, Philip Melanchthon was the first person in the history of biblical interpretation to analyze the rhetorical structure of Romans—that is, how Paul actually constructed his argument and the way that, rhetorically speaking, he organized his thoughts.[12]

10. Gottfried Arnold, *Unparteiische Kirchen- und Ketzer-geschichte* (Frankfurt/Main: Thomas Fritsch, 1700), 554.

11. As we shall examine in more detail in chapter 5, the New Perspective on Paul, similar to the Holy Roman Empire, is neither new nor Pauline. It is not new because Jerome and Erasmus, both of whose interpretations of Paul were well known to the Reformers, had already said much of what this group claims today to be "new." It is not Pauline because, were Paul's chief concern simply some arcane Jewish religious rules, he would never have used such outlandish language as "dying to the law" (Gal. 2) or spoken of his continued struggle against the law of coveting (Rom. 7). See Erik Heen, "A Lutheran Response to the New Perspective on Paul," *Lutheran Quarterly* 24 (2010): 263–91.

12. On Philip Melanchthon, see Timothy J. Wengert, "Philip Melanchthon's 1522 Annotations on Romans and the Lutheran Origins of Rhetorical Criticism," in *Biblical Interpretation in the Era of the Reformation*, ed. Richard A. Muller and John L. Thompson (Grand Rapids: Eerdmans, 1996), 118–40.

But this method also assumed something else that, in many ways, had been neglected or even forgotten by previous generations of exegetes. Humanists assumed that when analyzing a book the reader could figure out what the main point was. Thus, they looked for the *argumentum*, the basic point or argument, for each of the biblical books. This was true for Erasmus, John Calvin, and the Wittenberg Reformers. What Luther and Melanchthon argued, then, was that Scripture itself contained such an *argumentum* or *scopus*—namely, the book of Romans. Here they differed from other humanists, notably Erasmus, who imported into his interpretation of the New Testament a host of moralistic "nestlets," as he called them, cubbyholes (borrowed mostly from Cicero and other pagan ethicists) into which he shoved the various texts of the Bible. Here was a text on fasting; there was one on chastity; here was another on honesty; there were some on patience. Thus, when he came to Romans, Erasmus said that the first eleven chapters had to do with Paul's fight over circumcision and really did not apply to Erasmus's readers. Instead, he concentrated on Romans 12–15, where Paul presented his ethics.

Luther and Melanchthon viewed things in a radically different light. Paul in Romans provided *and intended to provide*, in Luther's words, the summary of the whole gospel: that we are justified by faith alone without the works of the law. This was what God had been up to since the garden of Eden, since Cain and Abel. Erasmus's interpretation was simply more James (that is, more law) and very little Christ, except that he imagined Christ was a new Moses, giving moral instruction to his "soldiers," as Erasmus called them.[13] Against this very approach Luther formulated the preface to his translation of Romans in the German New Testament.

> This epistle is the real main point of the New Testament and the very purest gospel. It is truly worthwhile for a Christian not only to memorize it word for word but also daily to walk with it as with the daily bread of the soul. For it can never be read or investigated too much or too well. The more it is used, the more priceless it becomes and the better it tastes.[14]

13. One of his most popular works was the *Enchiridion militis Christiani* (*Handbook of a Christian Soldier*).
14. WA DB 7:3, 1–11 (=LW 35:367).

In this same preface, Luther defined the major terms. Grace, he wrote, was (as Erasmus had already discovered about the Greek word *charis* and stated in his *Annotations to the New Testament*) God's favor and mercy. Sin was not simply our misdeeds but what stood deep in our hearts: our love and trust of self. And faith was not a human dream or projection, not a human work or decision, but

> a divine work in us that changes us, a new birth from God (John 1:12), and the death of the old creature that makes us an entirely different creature in heart, nerve, senses, and all powers and brings the Holy Spirit along with it. O, there is a living, creating, active, mighty thing surrounding faith in that it is impossible that it should not continually be working good. . . . Faith is a lively, active trust in God's grace, so certain that it would die a thousand times for it. And such trust and knowledge of God's grace makes a person joyful, bold, and happy toward God and all creatures—something that the Holy Spirit does in faith. . . . Pray God to work such faith in you, otherwise you will remain eternally without faith, no matter what you can or want to imagine or do. Such faith is righteousness and is called God's righteousness, which is reckoned as righteousness before God because it is God's gift.[15]

This is the heart of the matter, and it is why "Lutheran" exegetes, in the manner we have defined them above, are a dying breed. All Scripture rests on God's declaration of righteousness in Christ received by faith alone or, to use Luther's words, it goes back to faith that gives God what is owed to God—namely, all honor, glory, and righteousness. Suddenly, it is no longer human beings who work on becoming righteous to please God, but instead God holds all the cards and we repent in dust and ashes, clothed in Christ's righteousness alone. There it is. There really is a center to Scripture, and Paul in Romans is it. Our Christian lives are neither about fulfilling the law nor simply about setting aside some quaint Jewish ceremonies so that we can replace them with Christian ones. Our lives are hidden with Christ in God, clothed with Christ's righteousness, and Luther and Melanchthon's foolish claim that this is the center of the entire New Testament (and, indeed, the entire Bible) is still the heart of it all. We

15. WA DB 7:10, 6–29 (=LW 35:370–71).

are justified by faith alone without the works of the law. Applying the theology of the cross to Scripture results precisely in claiming *this* canon within the canon: God, the Just One, justifying the ungodly; Christ dying for sinners; relationship with God and the Christian life lived by faith alone.

Finding the Center of the Gospels

But there are other ways to use this Renaissance insight tempered by the theology of the cross and thus to discover not only the center of the Bible, the "Riddle of the New Testament" as Hoskyns and Davey called it,[16] but also the riddle or *argumentum*—main point—of other books as well. Since many pastors often preach on the appointed Gospels most Sundays, we will use Luther and Melanchthon's insight to examine these four books. In the present ecumenical three-year system of appointed texts, readings concentrate on one of the synoptic Gospels each year with the Gospel of John scattered throughout the three-year cycle.[17] To be sure, reading from the appointed texts is an "undifferentiated matter" (*adiaphoron*). But using such a lectionary demonstrates that each congregation is not alone since Christian assemblies all over the country and, indeed, the world and in many different denominations are united, reading the same lessons on the same day.[18] Thus, this common reading is a splendid external sign of the church's unity. Even Luther kept the readings of the medieval

16. Edwyn Hoskyns and Francis Davey, *The Riddle of the New Testament*, 3rd ed. (London: Faber & Faber, 1947). For a brilliant Lutheran approach to the Gospels, see Gordon W. Lathrop, *The Four Gospels on Sunday: The New Testament and the Reform of Christian Worship* (Minneapolis: Fortress, 2012).

17. For a strong defense for using the appointed Sunday texts, see Melinda Quivik, "Re-Assembly: Participation as Faith Construction," in *Centripetal Worship: The Evangelical Heart of Lutheran Worship*, ed. Timothy J. Wengert (Minneapolis: Augsburg Fortress, 2007), 47–65.

18. This was brought home to me in 2011, when the *Philadelphia Inquirer* described President Barack Obama's visit to a Washington, DC, congregation by mentioning only the Scripture passages read (to him and to me) that day. Lutheran exegetes and theologians who trumpet their freedom from such an ecumenical enterprise are simply reflecting their commitment to an approach gleaned from the Reformed tradition and are depriving students and parishioners of a far more evangelical way to read Scripture in the assembly.

one-year lectionary, refusing to change it (despite the fact that many Reformed churches did so) without consensus among all Christians. Such a consensus now exists. Moreover, for those who *do* attend church regularly, they and their fellow members will in three years hear a good chunk of the entire Bible read aloud. Of course, one can read these appointed texts in the assembly in such a hackneyed manner that no one wants to be there. But that is a matter of bad execution of good order and hardly reflects on the order itself. So, for those who do preach on the appointed lessons for Sunday, especially on the Gospels, the following may help them read and proclaim the Gospels through Luther's eyes.

The Gospel of Matthew is a hard nut to crack, since it is easy to read it in a moralistic manner. Many of the readings imply, and many commentaries unfortunately insist, that Matthew is the Gospel of the "New Law." There is the Sermon on the Mount in chapters 5–7, the woes to the Pharisees in chapter 23, and lots of instructions in between. Worse yet, Jesus says at the end, "Teaching them to observe all things *whatsoever I have commanded you.*" Sounds like more law! So some preachers committed to preaching God's grace hold their breath and wait for the years of Mark and Luke. Others simply batter their poor congregants with laws they cannot fulfill. In contrast to such skepticism, Philip Melanchthon's introduction to the Gospel of Matthew is far more gospel oriented and may easily apply to all the Gospels. He wrote:

> Always at the beginning of an exposition of books recounting the story of the Gospel, something must first be said about the distinction between law and gospel. Then, when something has been said about the promise, it must be added that these narrations have been written so that the apostles may be witnesses and posterity may be certain that the Messiah has been sent and manifested. Third, it may be stated that the Gospel reading principally consists of these four things: 1) stories about who Christ is and where he came from; 2) miracles testifying both that he is not an imposter but truly sent from God and that his teaching is true; 3) sermons on the gospel proper—that is, on the promises, such as: "All who believe in the Son will not perish" or "Come to me, all you who labor" and similar ones concerning eternal life; 4) sermons concerning good works, which are like sermons of

the law and interpretations of the law, and they pertain to sermons about repentance. And the distinction between precepts and promises must diligently be observed lest this light (that remission of sins is gratuitous) is lost.[19]

Melanchthon's careful distinction between law and gospel may be matched by the comments of the New Testament scholar Robin Mattison. To a perplexed professor of Reformation history (the author) who was preparing to lead a Bible study on Matthew, she once pointed out that understanding Matthew comes down to Matthew 1:21–23 (NRSV): "'She will bear a son, and you are to name him Jesus, for he will save his people from their sins.' All this took place to fulfill what had been spoken by the Lord through the prophet: 'Look, the virgin shall conceive and bear a son, and they shall name him Emmanuel,' which means, 'God is with us.'" The whole Gospel is about that one line: "God is with us."

Suddenly, armed with this one insight—this *argumentum* of Matthew's Gospel, so to speak—an entirely different face to the whole Gospel shows itself. If this is the heart and center of it all, then everything else in the Gospel revolves around this. For example, the end of the Gospel makes sense: "All authority in heaven and on earth has been given to me. . . . Look, I am with you always, even to the close of the age" (Matt. 28:18–20). God with us! Then the story of the wise men is about Messiah, who is God with us! And portions of the Sermon on the Mount are, indeed, law not gospel, being a second giving of the law by God to the people. "You have heard it said . . . but I say . . ."—that is, "You want a word that puts to death, try this one!" The people's comment about Jesus speaking with authority at the end of chapter 7 makes the point: this is God with us speaking and not a pious moralist!

But, within the Sermon on the Mount, there is remarkable gospel as well. Many treat the beatitudes like law—even Luther did in his brilliant exposition of them.[20] But, if this is God with us, then what we have here is Emmanuel speaking a law-breaking, death-defying promise. You see, the poor in heart, the meek, the peacemakers, those

19. CR 14:543–44.
20. WA 32:305–42 (=LW 21:10–53).

hungering and thirsting for righteousness, and all the rest—they are hardly happy, hardly blessed. Indeed, they are anything but! Yet Jesus declares—simply declares—that they are the blessed ones, and he promises what will happen to them.

Consider the beatitude addressed to those who grieve, "Blessed are those who mourn." No, sorry, Jesus! This is not true. Mourners are not blessed; they may be miserable, bereft, empty, hopeless, despairing, perhaps, but not blessed. The world may even call them cursed. Yet Jesus calls people the world views as weak and foolish to be the opposite. "God with us" simply declares something to be true that does not seem to be true. Why? Because they *will* be comforted—one day, on that "great gettin' up morning" in the words of the spiritual, when, as John Doberstein once put it, those sundered on earth shall foregather in heaven.[21] But the same is true of the other beatitudes as well.

With the Gospel of Mark, we have an easier time of it, especially if Roy Harrisville was right when he wrote *The Miracle of Mark*.[22] The Reformers did not have much to say about Mark, since they took it to be the *Reader's Digest* condensed version of Matthew. In the nineteenth century, however, scholars reached the conclusion that Mark was the first Gospel written and that Matthew and Luke came later. If there is a theologian of the cross among the Gospel writers, it is Mark. Here is the *gospel* of Jesus Christ, the Son of God, as the first verse announces, inventing an entirely new genre of literature with its use of the word *gospel*. Yet, as the story unfolds, we are confronted with the Son of God in the last place we would reasonably look, believed in by people whom we would scarcely have picked had we had any say in it. First, we have this rather odd character named John, baptizing in the wilderness. Then demons are the first to let the secret out, shouting in the synagogue. Then some cripple—using that word to reflect society's historical contempt of people who are lame—gets dropped through the roof, and Jesus, in a sure sign of blasphemy, pronounces forgiveness rather than simply healing him. On the way,

21. John Doberstein, ed., *A Minister's Prayer Book* (Philadelphia: Muhlenberg, 1959), 46. As a widower since May 18, 2001, I have also lived by that promise.
22. Roy A. Harrisville, *The Miracle of Mark* (Minneapolis: Augsburg, 1967). Harrisville reads the entire Gospel as a sermon on the Christ hymn in Phil. 2, which moves from his humiliation to exaltation as the crucified Son of God.

in chapter 4, we have Jesus talking in parables so that people will *not* believe. Now there is a scandal! Mark 8, smack dab in the middle of the Gospel, describes Peter, who musters up the "right answer" only to blow it when confronted by the cross. "Get behind me, Satan," Jesus says to Peter in contempt.

Mark 9 provides one of the favorite verses of both Philip Melanchthon and Martin Luther. It happens in the father's response when told by Jesus that only faith would help his little boy: "Lord, I believe; help my unbelief" (v. 24). There is the *simul iustus et peccator* (at the same time righteous and sinner), as clearly put as Paul does in Romans 7:19: "The good that I would, that I do not; the evil that I would not, that I do." But here it is *simul credens et incredens*, at the same time believing and unbelieving! The Christian believer lives in the midst of *Anfechtung*—that is, under assault or attack.[23] Doubt is not the opposite of faith; indeed, only believers may doubt! The opposite of faith *in Christ* (one has to add the object of faith at this point) is faith in the self, just what the father confesses he does not have. It is the same *simul* that Mark puts at the end of his Gospel, where the only believer at the cross, believe it or not, is a Roman centurion, exclaiming, "Truly this is the Son of God," right after the cry of dereliction. Then he leaves us with the women running pell-mell away from the tomb, filled with fear and telling no one—except, of course, they must have told someone, because here we are, worshipers of the same crucified and resurrected One.

So the lectionary gives us a year of preaching "God Is with Us," followed by a year of "The Son of God in the Last Place We Would Reasonably Look." Instead of using sermons to get people to volunteer to be on committees and give more money or to tell funny stories or to share their feelings, what would happen if pastors preached just the center of those texts for two years? Every text in the first two Gospels can be brought back to that center—mind you, not a center we choose but the center that the evangelists themselves proclaim.

Then comes the Gospel of Luke. This is the Gospel of Salvation *for You*. We hear this all over the place in Luke, but most especially

23. See Timothy J. Wengert, *Martin Luther's Catechisms: Forming the Faith* (Minneapolis: Fortress, 2009), 86–97.

in the famous line to the shepherds in Luke 2:11: "For to you is born this day in the city of David a savior, which is Christ the Lord." *To you!* And in chapter 1 Mary gets the same message from the angel and sings it in the Magnificat—with dumb Zechariah providing the basso profundo just a few verses later in the Benedictus.

One of the places to see the "For-you-ness" of this Gospel is in all the uniquely Lukan parables, although we tend to turn to the law when interpreting them. Consider three of the most famous. The parable of the good Samaritan (Luke 10:25–37) surely preaches the law when it makes all of those in need our neighbors, regardless of family origin. But, were the preacher to ask "who is this good Samaritan," what would happen? The more literally we take this parable, the more such candidates for the job of good Samaritan slowly disappear until there is only one left standing: our Lord Jesus Christ, who finds us beaten (in part by the law of this very parable) and dying on the side of the road, puts us up in the inn of the church, provides us with the two sacraments, and promises to return to pay all of our debts. Of course, some might imagine that this is rank allegorizing, which would be the case—but *only* if the parable did not work the law on the hearers and condemn them, eliminating every other candidate for "good Samaritan"! In any case, Luther too never failed to refer to the ancient church's allegory of this parable in his own sermons. Luke understood the stakes when he added the words "But wanting to justify himself, he asked . . ." (Luke 10:29 NRSV). This parable is thus aimed at the self-justifying old creature who is always out to minimize the law, to make it something it can fulfill. Once the law of this parable does its work, then the hearers are lying helpless on the side of the road in desperate need of a Savior.[24]

The parable of the prodigal son (Luke 15:11–32), as Helmut Thielicke pointed out years ago, is misnamed (by elder brothers, no

24. For a similar approach to Christ fulfilling the commandments, see the LC, Ten Commandments, 317, in BC, 429: "I say this repeatedly in order that we may get rid of the pernicious abuse that has become so deeply rooted and still clings to everyone, and so that all classes of people on earth may accustom themselves to look only at these precepts and heed them. It will be a long time before people produce a doctrine or social order equal to that of the Ten Commandments, for they are beyond human power to fulfill. The one who does fulfill them is a heavenly, angelic person, who is far above all holiness on earth."

doubt) and should be called the parable of the waiting father.[25] But even that is not quite right; it is the parable of the *running* father, who both runs out to meet the prodigal and comes out of the house a second time to invite the elder brother to the banquet. Indeed, taken literally, the two brothers are caught in precisely the same trap: neither believes that they are their father's sons. The younger brother practices on the way home, "I am not worthy to be your son; make me a slave" (15:19). (This, by the way, is good reason not to turn the earlier line, "he came to his senses," into some sort of decision to accept Jesus or to repent of his sins—he is deep in unbelief until the father calls him what he is not and cannot believe he could ever be again: his living, found son. The prodigal's reason allows him to be a slave; only the father's mercy calls him son.) And the elder son says, "All these years I have *slaved* for you" (15:29), hardly the words of a son and heir! To both sons the father declares the opposite to be the case: "This son of mine," he says about the youngest (15:24). "My son, all that is mine is yours," he confesses to the eldest (15:31). When people wonder what the elder son did after the father spoke to him, it only goes to show that they have no idea what the parable is about. When the father calls these two sinners sons, that is all there is to say. What elder and younger sons (and most later interpreters) cannot believe is precisely this: that the father's promise is for them!

The story of the tax collector and Pharisee (Luke 18:9–14) is another great example of the "for you" in Luke. Here the one whose religion is all about himself and his accomplishments goes home self-righteous but not justified, and the one who has no hope has, by his very confession of sin and begging for mercy, justified God's judgment and thereby goes home righteous simply by being declared righteous by Jesus ("I tell you, this man . . ."). Thus it is not the man's sorrow but Jesus' unexpected pronouncement that justifies the true sinner.

There are many other Lukan parables that do the same thing, but these three are more than enough to show that Luke announces the amazing word that salvation is *for you*. No wonder Jesus says from the cross in Luke, "Father, forgive them; they do not know what they

---

25. Helmut Thielicke, *The Waiting Father: Sermons on the Parables of Jesus*, trans. John W. Doberstein (New York: Harper, 1959). The English title was actually the suggestion of Doberstein.

are doing" (23:34), and Luther, preaching on this text in 1529 added, "Under the word, 'Father, forgive them,' I must count myself among the number of sinners for whom he prays."[26]

Philip Melanchthon's favorite verse in this Gospel was in Luke 24, where Luke tips his hand and reveals what the entire Gospel and the entire Bible are all about. "He opened their minds to understand the scriptures, and he said to them, 'Thus it is written, that the Messiah is to suffer and to rise from the dead on the third day, and that repentance and forgiveness of sins is to be proclaimed in his name to all nations, beginning from Jerusalem. You are witnesses of these things'" (24:45–48 NRSV). There it is, as clearly stated as anywhere in the New Testament: Jesus' death and resurrection matched with our death and resurrection—that is, with repentance (the death of the old) and forgiveness (the birth of the new). We find Melanchthon citing this verse three times in the Apology of the Augsburg Confession alone, including this précis: "The sum of the preaching of the gospel is to condemn sin and to offer the forgiveness of sins, righteousness on account of Christ, the Holy Spirit, and eternal life, so that having been reborn we might do good. Christ includes this in a summary of the gospel when he says in the last chapter of Luke: 'that repentance and forgiveness of sins is to be proclaimed in my name to all nations.'"[27] What is this but Melanchthon's way of saying Jesus Christ is for us, not against us?

Finally, we come to the Gospel of John, Martin Luther's favorite. It is, by John's own admission, the Gospel of faith. Already in his *Christmas Postil*, published in 1522, Luther pointed to John 1:12 as the point of the entire Gospel: "But to those who receive him, who believe in his name, he gives power to become the children of God."[28] We receive Jesus not by works but by faith alone. This fiercely faith-filled view of John was echoed first by Philip Melanchthon in his 1523 commentary,[29] but even more remarkably by one of Luther and Melanchthon's favorite

26. WA 29:241, 1–2, 25–26 (cf. Martin Luther, *The 1529 Holy Week and Easter Sermons of Dr. Martin Luther*, trans. Irving L. Sandberg [St. Louis: Concordia, 1999], 106).

27. Ap XII.29–30, in BC, 191–92.

28. WA 10/1/1:228, 3 (=LW 52:75).

29. See Timothy J. Wengert, *Philip Melanchthon's* Annotationes in Johannem *in Relation to Its Predecessors and Contemporaries* (Geneva: Librairie Droz, 1987), especially chapter 6.

students, Caspar Cruciger Sr., whom Luther called his Elisha. Cruciger's parents had moved from Leipzig to Wittenberg when he was young, and he began his studies there in the early 1520s. By the mid-1520s he had married an escaped nun, Elizabeth von Meseritz, whose hymn of Christ was printed in the first Protestant hymnbook of 1524 and is still in many Lutheran hymnals, including *Evangelical Lutheran Worship* (no. 309). He taught in Magdeburg's Latin school under Nicholas von Amsdorff for a time before returning in the 1530s to receive his doctorate in theology and teach alongside Luther.

In 1546 Cruciger published his commentary on the Fourth Gospel, probably based on notes provided to him by Melanchthon. In the *argumentum*, in which he spelled out the center of the book, Cruciger became the first exegete ever to argue in the very beginning of his commentary for what we take as a matter of course: that John 20:30–31 is the main point of the entire Gospel. "These things are written so that you may come to believe that Jesus is the Messiah, the Son of God, and through believing you may have life in his name."[30]

The alternative reduces the Gospel of John to philosophical arguments about the divinity of Christ. Indeed, Melanchthon himself in his commentary of 1523 mentioned that there were many who thought that all John has to do with is proving the divinity of Christ over against those who denied it, such as the so-called Ebionites, whom Melanchthon (incorrectly) thought were John's actual opponents around AD 90. To show the soteriological edge to the Gospel, Melanchthon wrote in his introduction, "That person is an Ebionite who denies that Jesus is the Son of God; but that person is twice an Ebionite who, while confessing that Jesus is the Son of God, denies his benefits."[31] For John, the point is not simply that Jesus, like God in Exodus 6, says "I am," but that he adds: "I am the bread of life, the gate, the shepherd, the resurrection and the life, the way, the truth and the life, and the vine." Truly, this Gospel is the Gospel of believing, of making people believers, and every last word relates to this center.

In addition, John develops a theology of the cross as a complement to Mark's, and yet in some ways it is so paradoxical that the reader

---

30. CR 15:7.
31. Quoted in Wengert, *Philip Melanchthon's* Annotationes in Johannem, 149.

can scarcely bear it. When Jesus announces, "Unless you eat the flesh of the Son of Man and drink his blood" (6:53 NRSV), many preachers retreat to the relatively safe confines of the Eucharist. But the likes of Augustine, Thomas Aquinas, and Martin Luther argued that John 6 had to do with eating by faith and that the mention of Christ's flesh and blood had to do with his flesh and blood on the cross. The true scandal—even the scandal behind the Lord's Supper itself—is the crucified I Am, who says, "And the bread that I will give for the life of the world is my flesh" (John 6:51 NRSV).

When he proclaims in John 7:38 that from "his side shall flow rivers of living water," Jesus is not talking about believers, as the NRSV ineptly translates by making the singular "his" into an inclusive "their." John has in mind Christ's actual wounded side, from which blood and water will flow. This is the place from which the Spirit comes, as is clear when the resurrected One, with nail prints in his hands and a spear wound in his side, breathes on his disciples and says, "Receive the Holy Spirit" (20:22). This is the living water of Jesus' encounter with the Samaritan woman at the well.

John 9:41 turns the world of the sightseeing Pharisees upside down by proclaiming, "Because you say, 'we see,' you are blind." Indeed, there is so much paradox in John, so much of God's revelation in the last place one would reasonably look, that the reader, the preacher, and the hearer are all forced to believe in the One who, when he is lifted up on the cross, is glorified, draws all to himself, and provides living water for a thirsty world. There is no place for works here, not even in the definition of faith, so that Jesus says (in John 6:44), "no one can come to me unless the Father draws him." Perhaps George Herbert knew what John was up to when he wrote, "Come my Way, my Truth, my Life. Such a Way as gives us breath; such a Truth as ends all strife; such a Life as killeth death."[32]

So, like it or not, Luther, Melanchthon, and those who are captured by their approach to Scripture teach encountering the center of that Scripture in weakness: the very weakness of the crucified and resurrected One, who pronounces the dead alive, the sinner forgiven, and the poor filled with good things. With Romans at the heart of their

32. George Herbert, "The Call," in *The Temple* (1633).

interpretation, such people confess that they are justified by faith in Jesus Christ alone and thus distinguish law and gospel. Then each Gospel comes to our aid: Matthew, the Gospel of "God with us"; Mark, proclaiming the Son of God in the last place we would reasonably look; Luke, announcing salvation *for us*; and John, the Gospel of faith in this crucified and risen Word made flesh. Then, by faith alone, the weak, foolish Word of the Gospels truly becomes the power of God and the wisdom of God.

4

Practice

Luther's Biblical Ethics

This chapter examines several of the basic premises of Martin Luther's biblical, grace-filled ethics: *Gleichmut*, *Gewissen*, and *Glaube*—that is, fairness, conscience, and faith. To these will then be added a fourth "G": *Gemeinschaft* (community). All of these arose out of Luther's remarkable encounter with God's Word in Scripture, the topic of the preceding chapters. As helpful as other scholars have been in describing Luther's ethics, much of what has been written on the subject since the mid-nineteenth century has been written from what one might call a theoretical perspective: moving from ethical principles to application. This approach can easily distort Luther's thought.

Consider the first Lutheran to write a book on ethics, Gottlieb Christoph Adolf von Harleß. In the seventh edition of his *Christliche Ethik* (*Christian Ethics*) published in 1875, von Harleß coined the phrase "orders of creation" (*Schöpfungsordnung*). To be sure, he used it specifically to indicate that this world's "orders" (government, household, and church) were human creations. He explained that he used this phrase "because even the best earthly order does not possess by definition immortality; the existing order is not unequivocally binding on the Christian."[1] Beginning in the twentieth century and continuing to the present, however, this same tentative label of human limitations had become in the minds and writings of other scholars a fixed, God-given category, coined by Luther (so many thought) and therefore unequivocally binding on Lutherans. By the 1950s, some argued that there were *heterosexual* orders of creation in Luther's thought as a way of preventing the ordination of women.[2] From such fixed, overarching categories, one then derives the consequences of ethical deliberation.

Nowhere is this movement from fixed forms to daily application more widespread than in Paul Althaus's classic description of Luther's ethics.[3] Using a technique similar to Philip Melanchthon's *loci communes* (commonplaces), Althaus divides his work into what he claims are the basic categories of Luther's thought and only on rare occasions examines Luther's practice. The problems with such approaches to Luther's ethics are manifold. Luther did not think in such categories and certainly did not act that way. That is, he did not begin with rigid principles and categories of behavior and then try to apply them to his circumstances. Quite the contrary, he was only too happy to criticize this very approach, one he associated rightly with the lawyers of his day and their growing preoccupation with Roman law, where (to this day) one does law by applying fixed categories to individual cases.[4] Luther's ethics, by contrast, were quite contextual. He was a moving ethical target, changing his approach to match what he thought best suited the situation. He therefore left his followers not with a set of ethical principles that they had to try to apply willy-nilly in their own day ("Luther said it; I believe it; that settles it") but

1. Gottlieb Christoph Adolf von Harleß, *Christliche Ethik*, 7th ed. (Gütersloh: Bertelsmann, 1875), 491.

2. For a description of the development of this term in American Lutheranism, see Christian Batalden Scharen, *Married in the Sight of God: Theology, Ethics and Church Debates over Homosexuality* (Lanham, MD: University Press of America, 2000), 55–92.

3. Paul Althaus, *The Ethics of Martin Luther*, trans. Robert C. Schultz (Philadelphia: Fortress, 1972).

4. For Luther's comments on law and lawyers, see James Estes, "Luther's Attitude toward the Legal Traditions of His Time," *Luther-Jahrbuch* 76 (2009): 77–110.

rather with an approach to life itself that forces believers to wrestle with the same ethical issues that Luther confronted and then come to their own conclusions.

Rule-based ethics often removes Christians from having to take responsibility for their neighbor's actions and for their own actions vis-à-vis the neighbor, since one can always hide behind the safety of following orders despite harm to the neighbor. And such an approach allows people to place the blame for bad actions or advice on others, even on the Lawgiver. "Am I my brother's keeper?" (Gen. 4:9) and "The woman whom you gave me, she made me do it" (Gen. 3:12) are the two earliest examples in the Bible of this failed ethic. "Who is my neighbor?" (Luke 10:29) is yet a third. To avoid this rule-based approach, Luther's actions mapped out patterns of behavior toward the neighbor that Luther himself consistently followed as he approached ethical dilemmas in his day.

Gleichmut: The Christian's Balancing Act

A very important term in Luther and Melanchthon's ethical deliberations is *Gleichmut*.[5] They actually knew and labeled it by its Greek name, *epieikeia*, or its Latin equivalent, *aequitas*. In fact, the transliterated Greek word actually found its way into many German texts, including *The Book of Concord*.[6] *Epieikeia* is a technical term coined by Aristotle and used extensively by the Stoics in their ethical writings. Although the legal tradition translated it as "equity" or "fairness" (hence the Latin *aequitas*), a more accurate translation, especially for the way Luther and Melanchthon used it, would be "reasonableness" or "balance." Even the Latin *aequitas*, which means "fairness," had the connotation of moderation, equanimity, or proportion (balance). *Gleichmut* and the other German equivalents, which in later usage often meant simply "neutrality" or "impartiality," were such inaccurate renderings of the Greek that the Reformers often used the Greek term in German and even turned it into a German verb.

---

5. Sometimes they use other related terms such as *Billigkeit* or *Mildigkeit*.
6. See, for example, CA XXVI.14, in BC, 76.

Luther used this concept in the third, often overlooked, section of his famous tract *On Secular Authority*.[7] He wrote this part as a *Fürstenspiegel* (that is, a mirror for princes), which was a familiar genre of writing in the late Middle Ages, written for the instruction of the nobility. In this final, practical section, Luther summarized a Christian prince's behavior. First, he was not to imagine that the principality was his own, but rather he had to serve his people. Second, he should not trust the advice of the big shots (*grosse Hansen* [literally, big Hanses])—that is, his own counselors. Third, he had to punish evildoers appropriately; that is (in Luther's colorful language), he should be careful not to keep the soupspoon from dripping by spilling the entire bowl. One was not to punish injustice in such a way that it caused greater harm. Finally, Luther counseled his prince to judge using natural law or reason (what he even called "common sense") and love.

> For where you judge according to love, you will very easily determine everything and make judgments without any law books at all. As soon as you lose sight of love and natural law, you will come to conclusions that no longer please God, even if you swallowed every law book and every jurist whole. Instead, the more you think about them, the more they will make you err. A right good judgment must not and cannot be spoken out of books but rather from common sense [*aussz freyem synn*], as if there were no law books at all. But such a free judgment comes only from love and natural law of which reason itself is full. From books come only strained and wavering judgments.[8]

Here, without using the term, Luther described in detail what *Gleichmut*—reasonable behavior—looked like in a prince. It eschewed the narrowness of book law for the freedom of love and common sense, reason, and natural law. Quite frankly, this kind of freedom escapes most people. Most of us would prefer to throw the book at the neighbor rather than to use a more balanced, loving approach. In fact, such an approach to ethical dilemmas might well smack of a "situational ethic," which those accustomed to using a rule-based

7. WA 11:229–80 (=LW 45:75–129).
8. WA 11:279, 26–34 (=LW 45:128).

approach assiduously try to avoid. This approach also showed that for Luther, God had two hands. It was here, in this world, when dealing with the neighbor, that Christians could use Aristotle or anyone else—even Dr. Phil—to help solve ethical dilemmas. Love, natural law, and reason—not faith, gospel, and cross—were key to Luther's approach to ethics.

The late Franklin Drewes Fry—son of Franklin Clark Fry, who was president of the Lutheran Church in America and, before that, of the United Lutheran Church in America—coined a fine summary of this approach for his congregants. Pastor Fry had an amazing ability to summarize complicated Lutheran theological principles into compact, pithy sayings. In this case, he summarized Lutheran ethics by saying that in any moral dilemma, Lutherans are committed to giving it their "reverent, best guess." It is "reverent" in the sense that it is not based on selfish desires but on God's will for all human beings, what Luther called here natural law. Second, it is "best." That is, Christians apply their best reason in trying to figure out what they are to do. Sloppy ethical thinking, no matter how pious, does no one any good. Finally, it is a guess! Rather than deriving behavior from rigid principles, it must come from love—which means that Christians do not have the luxury of idolizing or idealizing what they do. Everything remains tentative, penultimate, and, thus, loving. This means those following this principle—even Luther himself—make mistakes, which is to be expected. We just dare not worship them.

Luther not only advised his prince to use such an approach; he also followed his own advice. The outrageous ethical suggestions he made and followed in the course of his life were not for others to follow in lockstep, as if he possessed some sort of infallibility. Instead, his very fallible behavior gives us leave to—using a phrase out of context—"sin boldly and believe more boldly still"—that is, to give it a reverent best guess.

Here are a few of the instances where Luther used *Gleichmut* to aid him in his own ethical deliberations. A woman marries a fellow, and he turns out unable to fulfill her sexually.[9] Against the entire tradition and all of our own most cherished Victorian mores, what did Luther

---

9. WA 10/2:278, 10–279, 6 (=LW 45:20–21); cf. WA 6:558 (=LW 36:103–5).

suggest? With the husband's assent—since he was basically dishonest in marrying her in the first place—the wife could find a replacement. Even in the sixteenth century, this advice was viewed as over the top. Yet that is what Luther suggested in print in 1523, defending an initial statement to that effect made in 1520.

The local imperial prince, the Landgrave Philip of Hesse, was married to someone (for dynastic reasons) whom he simply could not abide—among other things she really smelled (which in the sixteenth century must have been quite an odor). For years he had been living with Mechthild, but because he knew that this was adultery, he had been unwilling and unable to receive the Lord's Supper. Being a prince of the empire, he needed to go to the bishop of Rome for a divorce, who was not about to give the Protestant Prince Philip the time of day, let alone a legal separation. So what did Luther (along with Philip Melanchthon and Martin Bucer) suggest? Simple: bigamy! That is, a secret marriage to his lover. This solution unraveled, of course, when Mechthild insisted on wearing the crown in public, so to speak, but the very audacity of it was precisely the kind of *Gleichmut* Luther championed most.[10]

A much less well-known case occurred in 1535 and was only recently republished in the new edition of Philip Melanchthon's correspondence.[11] It was the kind of case that Wittenberg's theologians dealt with constantly once the Reformation did away with the old episcopal family courts in the 1520s: a man appealed to his pastor for permission to marry his cousin. As it turns out, the couple had already been "*eingebettet*" (that is, sleeping in the same bed) for three years and, not surprisingly, had a child together. The pastor turned to Wittenberg for advice. The Wittenberg theologians granted that Scripture did not strictly forbid such a marriage (look at the patriarchs!) but also that traditionally this was not the sort of thing one should condone in Germany. Their solution? Have the fellow thrown in jail for three weeks, and after that let the couple marry. This way, people would not follow his example (no one signed up for German jails in that era), but the child and mother would have a father and husband.

---

10. See Martin Brecht, *Martin Luther: The Preservation of the Church 1532–1546*, trans. James L. Schaaf (Minneapolis: Fortress, 1993), 205–15.
11. MBW 1411 (*Texte* 6:50–53).

It was just this kind of creative solution to the sexual dilemmas of the sixteenth century that got Luther in trouble with lawyers in the 1540s and resulted in some of his most caustic comments about them. In a sermon on the Feast of the Epiphany, 1544, Luther raged against "*die Juristen*," as he called them.[12] (In this sermon he also called them clumps of excrement hanging from the pope's arse.) Besides raging against secret engagements, which Luther insisted usually ended in secret annulments, Luther took the case where a judge knew for a certainty that a man was innocent and yet convicted him based on the testimony of several witnesses, as imperial (Roman) law demanded. Luther exploded:

> Dear judge, you should declare, "I find him innocent, despite the fact that there are 10,000 witnesses against him, since I know he is innocent. And if that is against the imperial (Roman) law? I shit on the imperial law that declares an innocent man guilty! Dear witnesses, you witness in favor of unfairness [he used an antonym for *Gleichmut*]." Think of how many false witnesses there have been in the world. Christ was crucified based on the testimony of false witnesses; Steven was stoned. Witnesses can be false. . . . The judge should say, "Because I know that this would be a miscarriage of justice, I cannot condemn him." Jurists have no conscience; therefore they do not ask about the *periculo conscientiae* [danger to the conscience].[13]

Das Gewissen: The Conscience

This final comment introduces a second category in Luther's ethical deliberations: the conscience. Some insist that the term only applied to matters of salvation in Luther's thought. In fact, however, the category of the "bound conscience" had a far wider application.[14] Of course,

12. WA 49:298, 25–27 and 299, 1–5.
13. WA 49:304, 29–38.
14. The concept of the bound conscience is not often used in ethical considerations of other Christian churches. However, in the Lutheran church, chiefly because of its history and its central theological principles, this concept does play an important part in ethics and pastoral care. Indeed, it highlights the pastoral underpinnings of Lutheran theology and the Lutheran rejection of both papalism and its individualistic equivalent, "*Enthusiasmus*," in ethical deliberation. The term *bound conscience*, which found use in recent proposals from the task force for ELCA Studies on Sexuality approved by the church-wide assembly in August 2009, has its origins both in the

Luther often did use the term in matters of salvation, but that does not tell the whole story. The word *Gewissen* or, in sixteenth-century German, *Konscientz*, was used in a variety of ways by the Reformers. To be sure, they rejected the binding of consciences to human traditions for obtaining salvation. But they also rejected binding consciences to any law—divine or human. The "terrified conscience" was indeed the point of contact between God and humanity, but through the law and wrath of God that terrified us. Comfort to the conscience came only through faith in God's unconditional, gracious promise of forgiveness in Christ. Luther's appeal in Worms to his bound conscience had to do not simply with the sense of right and wrong (as we use the term *conscience* today, as in "let your conscience be your guide") but also with the God-given conviction that Christ alone was Savior. Luther's concern for other "ensnared, vexed, and flayed" consciences had to do precisely with questions of salvation.[15]

In October 1518, when Martin Luther appeared in Augsburg before the papal legate, Cardinal Cajetan, he had already posted and defended the Ninety-Five Theses. His theological position had become a case before Rome. In deference to Luther's prince, Elector Frederick the Wise, Cajetan did not simply haul Luther off to Rome for summary judgment but interviewed him in Augsburg. Of the two points on which Cajetan faulted Luther's writings, one concerns us here. Cajetan insisted that one could never be certain about being in a state of grace but always had to doubt the words of absolution (to avoid being overcome with prideful security). Luther responded this way:

> May it please your highness to intercede with our most holy lord, Leo X, in my behalf so that he will not proceed against me with such stern rigor that he cast my soul into darkness, for I seek nothing but the light of truth and I am prepared to give up, change, or revoke everything if I am informed that these passages are to be understood

---

Pauline correspondence (Rom. 14–15 and 1 Cor. 6; 8–10) and in the early Lutheran appropriation of this term for use in the ethical dilemmas they faced. Both Luther and Melanchthon used the term *conscience* as describing the entire person standing before God and viewed in the light of God's Word, understood as law and gospel.

15. It is also important to note that for Luther the term *conscience* was not simply a certain faculty of the soul, as medieval theologians thought. He used the term to apply to the entire person convicted and comforted before God.

in another sense. For I am neither arrogant nor so eager for vainglory that for this reason I would be ashamed to revoke ill-founded doctrines. Indeed, it will please me most of all if the truth is victorious. However, I do not want to be compelled to affirm something contrary to my conscience, for I believe without the slightest doubt that this is the meaning of Scripture.[16]

Here Luther appealed to the pope and his representative as pastors to his own soul and begged them not to make him choose between Scripture and obedience to the Holy See. Thus, the bound conscience always appealed for comfort from those called to speak God's Word of promise and hope.

Three years later, Luther made similar statements before the emperor, Charles V, except that the matter was no longer open.

Since, then, your serene majesty and your lordships seek a simple answer, I will give it in this manner, neither horned nor toothed: unless I am convinced by the testimony of the Scriptures or by clear reason (for I do not trust either in the pope or in the councils alone, since it is well known that they have often erred and contradicted themselves), I am bound by the Scriptures I have quoted and my conscience is captive to the Word of God. I cannot and I will not retract anything, since it is neither safe nor right to go against conscience.[17]

This notion that the Word of God, as heard by the sinner-declared-saint, bound the conscience to it serves as a warning not to dismiss summarily the person who makes such a claim. We are neither pope nor emperor but fellow believers living with one another. This means that Christians cannot simply assert one interpretation of Scripture over another but must always respect the conscience of others with whom we may disagree. If Luther had no choice but to appeal to the conscience bound to the gospel in his case before Rome, we should be all the more ready to respect cases of bound consciences regarding the lesser matters of law and ethics.

This position was for Luther not an easy one to hold. It was not, as later historians sometimes portrayed it, the first instance of a free,

16. Using the translation in LW 31:275 (=WA 2:16, 13–20).
17. As translated in LW 32:112 (=WA 7:838, 2–8).

enlightened conscience shedding the shackles of medieval religion. Luther's conscience was not free but bound to God's Word, which assured him of God's free and unconditional forgiveness in Christ. However, because of the vulnerable nature of such a position, Luther was often assaulted with *Anfechtung*, attacks of the devil, which tried to undermine his confidence by asking, "Are you alone right?" ("Bist du allein richtig?"). Those who claim that their conscience is bound to a particular interpretation of Scripture are encouraged by Luther's example likewise to demonstrate such humility and must anticipate doubts and struggles.

The events surrounding Luther's "case" hardly exhaust Luther's (or Melanchthon's) sensitivity to conscience. In March 1522, when Luther raced back to Wittenberg after nearly a year of protective custody in the Wartburg Castle, he encountered in Wittenberg people with weak consciences who were bound to believe that they sinned by receiving the cup in Communion or by taking the bread in their hands or by eating meat on fast days. Now, Luther did *not* say in his famous Invocavit sermons[18]—those eight sermons preached during the single week in March immediately after his return—that these bound consciences were correct. In fact, he made it quite clear that they were not correct. However, being right in faith (that is, holding the correct principles) did not mean that his radical coworkers (including not only Andreas Bodenstein von Karlstadt [later his bitter opponent over the Lord's Supper] but also Philip Melanchthon, Justus Jonas, and Nicholas von Amsdorff) were right in love.

What Luther was dealing with here was not a small matter; it was a dominical command ("Take and drink of it, *all* of you"), a Babylonian captivity of the sacrament by the Antichrist, as Luther himself had described it in 1520. And yet, for the sake of the weak, Luther went so far as to say that he would himself only eat bread and never take it in the hand. Of course, St. Paul had argued similarly in Romans and 1 Corinthians. There the matter was meat sacrificed to idols, which had to do with the first commandment. Such matters may look trivial today simply because they have been resolved. But in Luther's day, or

18. WA 10/3:1–64 (=LW 51:69–100). They were so called because he preached the first sermon on "Invocavit Sunday," the first Sunday in Lent, and the eighth one a week later.

in Paul's, they were matters of right and wrong and *at the same time* matters of salvation. Thus, Luther said to those insisting on change,

> I was glad to know when someone wrote me that some people here had begun to receive the sacrament in both kinds. You should have allowed it to remain thus and not forced it into a law. But now you go at it pell-mell, and headlong force every one to it. Dear friends, you will not succeed in that way.[19]

In the case of the church visitation of 1527, Philip Melanchthon inspected a cloister where the nuns had two complaints.[20] They criticized their preacher, who kept instructing them to take Communion in both kinds, and, not surprisingly, they protested having to receive the sacrament in both kinds. Melanchthon's solution? The preacher stayed, but the nuns did not have to receive the cup, since it violated their conscience. That is, they had to hear the truth of Christ's command, "Take and drink of it, all of you," but they could not be forced to receive the cup against their conscience. This exception granted to these nuns was so important that the Reformers wrote it into the German Visitation Articles, published in 1528.

> Inasmuch, however, as no one is to be forced to believe, or driven by command or force from his unbelief, since God likes no forced service and wants only those who are his servants by their own free will, and in view of the fact that the people are confused and uncertain, it has been and still is impossible to establish a rule concerning persons to whom both kinds are to be offered or from whom they are to be withheld according to the teaching of Christ.[21]

In what followed, Luther and Melanchthon outlined what should be done. "But as this article arises daily and troubles the conscience, we have not wanted to leave the pastors without any guidance at all."[22] They were to teach the true doctrine, but

19. Using the translation in LW 51:91 (=WA 10/3:46, 21–26).
20. See MBW 567 (*Texte*, 3:112–13), dated July 29, 1527.
21. Using here and in what follows the translation in LW 40:290 (=WA 26:214, 15–20). This exception to Communion in both kinds continued in force for at least ten years.
22. LW 40:290 (=WA 26:214, 28–29).

where there are weak Christians, who as yet have not heard or been suf-
ficiently instructed and strengthened by the word of the gospel, and so
out of weakness and terror of conscience rather than obstinacy cannot
receive both kinds, one may allow these to take Communion in one
kind. . . . In this way the doctrine of both kinds will not be weakened
or compromised, but only the application or use of the doctrine will
be temporarily postponed through Christian patience and love.[23]

They compared this approach to the patience of Christ, who tolerated
both the apostles' desire to call down fire from heaven (Luke 9:54–56)
and their quarreling over which one was superior (Matt. 20:20–28).
They added, "Further, it is uncharitable, even un-Christian, to force
these weak ones to receive the sacrament in both kinds or to withhold
it in one kind. For thus they feel they are made to sin."[24]

Of course, some were not weak but merely obstinate. "The pastor,
who knows his people and daily associates with them, must distinguish between the weak and the obstinate."[25] Although the question
of Communion using both bread and wine might seem to us like a
small matter, nevertheless for the people involved this was a problem
of the highest importance, involving the conflict between Christ's
clear command and pastoral care for the bound conscience. Concern
for the bound conscience here was not simply toleration for different
points of view but rather a realization that the neighbor's conscience
was bound to a totally different, albeit incorrect, understanding of the
matter and that to uproot that understanding would have shaken the
neighbor's faith and trust in God's mercy and forgiveness.

Ten years later, and then only under pressure, the Reformers agreed
to remove this clause. When Melanchthon's former student Jakob
Schenck attacked him for dragging his feet on Communion in both
kinds at that time, Melanchthon wrote a scathing oration, dripping
with sarcasm and delivered by one of his students to the entire Wittenberg university community, entitled, "On the Ingratitude of the
Cuckoo."[26]

23. LW 40:290–91 (=WA 26:214, 37–215, 6).
24. LW 40:291 (=WA 26:215, 18–20).
25. LW 40:292 (=WA 26:216, 1–2).
26. See CR 11:335–42.

The appeal to the bound conscience was not a matter of these early, "freethinking" Lutherans claiming that their own consciences were bound to their particular way of determining right and wrong. Instead, it was up to those who were in authority and who had determined that, indeed, such behavior was *wrong* to discern in their weak neighbors a conscience bound to a different understanding of Scripture and practice. That is to say, the business of determining the difference between a bound, perhaps weak, conscience and a stubborn one fell in the laps of those in authority who disagreed, who were certain that such behavior was wrong—that is, those who were the strong. It was thus a matter of appealing to, or begging, those authorities (who were certain that such behavior was wrong) to have mercy on those in the church who could not imagine that such behavior was what the Bible was talking about and therefore who supported a different position.[27]

Luther's concern for the weak conscience was not limited just to practices surrounding the Lord's Supper. He could also set aside other divine commandments for the sake of those to whom he was pastor. The New Testament allowed for divorce only in the case of adultery. Luther dealt with specific matters of sexual behavior in his tract *On the Estate of Marriage*.[28] As noted above, there he defended his suggestion that the wife of a man unable to fulfill his conjugal duty should be able to contract a secret marriage to another and thus bear children. In another instance, Luther counseled soldiers about refusing to serve in an unjust war.[29] Here, as in his 1523 writing *On Temporal Authority*, Luther emphasized the role of equity in governing.[30] In particular, he left the determination of a just or unjust war not under the purview of religious leaders but in the soldiers' own hands.[31]

27. In some ways, many ethical debates today are not as serious as Luther's willingness to overlook a dominical command for the sake of the weak conscience. More often than not we do not actually debate whether a biblical command is valid but rather whether it is valid in a particular circumstance. Those who refused to receive the cup were resisting a dominical command per se.
28. WA 10/2:267–304 (=LW 45:11–49).
29. *Whether Soldiers, Too, Can Be Saved* from 1526; WA 19:616–63 (=LW 46:87–137).
30. WA 19:645, 6–655, 5 (=LW 45:118–29).
31. WA 19:656, 22–657, 10 (=LW 46:130–31).

Finally, as mentioned above, Luther and Melanchthon suggested to Landgrave Philip of Hesse, who was staying away from the Lord's Supper because he was living with another woman, that he should commit bigamy rather than divorce his wife—advice that the prince followed (with unfortunate consequences).[32] In all of these cases, Luther and Melanchthon behaved with a kind of ethical freedom rarely practiced today. For them, in pastoral issues, the individual conscience, freedom in Christ's forgiveness, and the right use of reason (balance) in specific cases outweighed slavish adherence to laws.

In any case, Luther respected the human conscience far more than many folks give him credit. He gave to citizens the right to flee an unjust ruler. He refused to turn pastors into mini-popes, determining right and wrong and fixing the terms of salvation for their flock. Instead, he was always fighting for the endangered conscience. For Luther one could not simply make rules and figure that that fulfilled one's pastoral duty. Christians had to minister to the souls and consciences and bodies of real people. This meant giving it a reverent best guess to try to free folks from whatever prisons of conscience they had fallen into.

Scott Hendrix puts it somewhat differently. He writes, "An appeal to the Reformation would argue, however, that Lutherans are free to disagree not because our consciences are bound in the modern sense but because they are free in the Reformation sense—that is, not because our consciences are bound to personal convictions that may invoke Scripture but because they are liberated in Christ from additional requirements for salvation."[33] To comprehend fully Luther's pastoral ethic, one need only add that such freed consciences are then bound to take special care for those with whom they disagree—and not merely by saying that they hate the sin but love the sinner—by showing true, deep, meaningful respect for those who seem not to be as free as they themselves are, for the weak and terrified consciences in their care. And this advice works both ways.

---

32. In another case, Luther speculated that perhaps an adulterous divorced person could move to a far country and remarry, if the desire for companionship was too strong to resist.

33. Scott Hendrix, "Homosexuality, Conscience, and the Reformation," *Lutheran Partners* (July/August 2005): 30–31.

Even disagreeing with a particular application of the category of conscience in Luther's thought does not mean throwing baby Martin out with the bathwater. Luther is not here to serve as pope but as pastoral example. There are countless cases where sensitivity to the boundedness of the neighbor's conscience remains an important pastoral tool. This is especially true for all of those fights in which parishes become entangled over *adiaphora*—matters where we cannot differentiate between good and evil or right and wrong. Whether it is the color of the wallpaper in the men's bathroom, the size of Communion glasses, the frequency of Communion, what kind of robes we wear, or where the choir stands, one may use the Formula of Concord and its profound guidelines to help us sort out the problems.[34] Christian assemblies, which have the right to change such practices as they see fit, may set things up for good order in service of the gospel but in such a way as not to offend the weak. One is free in ethical considerations to serve the gospel, to maintain good order, and to protect the weak. Would that every Lutheran church council could memorize article 10 of the Formula! Imagine congregations founded on the principle that no one gets to pontificate, but everyone gets to look out for their neighbor's conscience.

Glaube: Faith

If questions of balance and conscience relate to law and pastoral care, respectively, we now come to the heart of it all: the gospel itself. Christians are justified by faith alone. Some may immediately correct this statement, based on some memory of article 4 of the Augsburg Confession, and say, "out of grace for Christ's sake through faith." To be sure, that is what Philip Melanchthon wrote in article 4 of the Augsburg Confession.[35] He put the expanded version of the same thing, however, in article 20.

> Our works cannot reconcile God or merit grace and forgiveness of sins, but we obtain this only *by* faith when we believe that we are received

34. See Timothy J. Wengert, *A Formula for Parish Practice: Using the Formula of Concord in Congregations* (Grand Rapids: Eerdmans, 2006), 165–79.
35. CA IV.1 (German), in BC, 38, 40.

into grace on account of Christ, who alone has been appointed mediator and atoning sacrifice through whom the Father is reconciled.[36]

The emphasis on "only" and "alone" in article 20 is where it belongs
in our ethical deliberations: not simply on a definition of grace as
God's mercy but rather on faith and trust in Christ.

The first thing to note here is that Melanchthon contrasted faith
with works. We live in a nation where, for most Christians, faith and
works have become hopelessly entangled. Most congregants believe
that the faith that justifies us is itself a work, a decision that human
beings undertake in order to jump-start the entire mechanism of grace.
Against this cultural confusion, the Augsburg Confession and Luther's
Small Catechism insist that faith is *not* a human work; faith is what
God the Holy Spirit works in human beings through the hearing of the
good news of God in Christ. "I believe that by my own understanding
or strength I cannot believe in Jesus Christ my Lord or come to him,
but the Holy Spirit has called me through the gospel," Luther cried
out in the explanation to the third article of the Apostles' Creed.[37]
In America, where everything depends on what we do, few hold this
position. Few churches claim both the centrality of the means of grace
("through the gospel") and the giftedness of faith ("I cannot believe")
quite the way Luther does.

Second, it is (in the Latin text especially) *by* faith. Although sometimes faith seems to be an instrument, the human side to the faith/
grace equation, so that the confessors could sometimes write "through
faith," the true scandal in the Augsburg Confession comes when Melanchthon writes not *per fidem* (through faith) but *fide* (by faith).[38]
Then, with faith clearly *not* a work to do or a decision to make, hu-
mans are faced with a proposition guaranteed to kill the old creature,
who is always looking for a way to stay in control of spiritual matters:
human beings are not in charge of their relation to God; God is. And
the contours of that relation are not the works of a robust conscience

36. CA XX.9 (Latin), in BC, 54, emphasis added.
37. SC, Creed, 6, in BC, 355.
38. Because in sixteenth-century German the preposition *durch* can mean either
"by" or "through" (i.e., either efficient or instrumental cause), the Latin is clearer,
since it uses *per fidem* for "through faith" and, as here, the simple ablative case *fide*
for "by faith."

but, to quote Melanchthon later in the same article, "trust that consoles and encourages terrified minds."

Third, grace is not stuff. It is not a power or force. Even if they have watched all the episodes of Star Wars, Christian pastors and leaders dare not say about grace, "The force be with you," and imagine that they have said anything very profound or Christian. Luther grew up in a world where grace was a power that came in basically two forms. For people in a state of sin there was *gratia gratis data*, grace given freely. Most theologians argued that this offer of grace came in sermons that encouraged sinners to partake in the sacrament of penance to move into a state of grace. This was grace as information, not unlike the way grace is often dished out today in revivalist churches or their descendants. Gabriel Biel, the late-medieval thinker whom Luther read assiduously as a young student, even argued that such grace was simply the human powers to love God and neighbor while still in a state of sin, a position that the Reformation historian Stephen Ozment once described as Augustinian form with Pelagian content.[39]

Once one went to the sacrament of penance, or was truly sorry for sin out of love of God (the first step in penance), a second form of grace was poured into the penitent, and that was the *gratia gratum faciens*, the grace that makes acceptable to God. This was an infused habit, or disposition, hardwired directly into the human soul. Similar kinds of grace came in other sacraments, such as the indelible character of ordination. Any time one turns grace into a power like this, however, its gracious character gets lost.

What Luther and Melanchthon learned—from Erasmus of Rotterdam of all people—was that in the Greek New Testament the word translated into Latin as *gratia* or "grace" was χάρις, which means *favor Dei*, "the favor of God" or, as the Reformers would later prefer, *misericordia Dei*, "the mercy of God."[40] Many in Luther's day said that people are saved by grace alone, in part because late-medieval theology believed everything, even meritorious works and human powers, to be

39. Related to the author by David C. Steinmetz.
40. Rolf Schäfer, "Melanchthon's Interpretation of Romans 5:15: His Departure from the Augustinian Concept of Grace Compared to Luther's," in *Philip Melanchthon (1497–1560) and the Commentary*, ed. Timothy J. Wengert and M. Patrick Graham (Sheffield: Sheffield Academic Press, 1997), 79–104.

a matter of God's "grace." However, when the Reformers simply said that our justification occurs "gratis," freely and from God's mercy alone, they were stating something so radical about grace that what they said eliminated all this talk about power. So, perhaps one should say, "May God's mercy be with you" or "God's mercy is with you," and leave it at that, which is exactly what the absolution is all about.

When Sunday school children learn that grace is God's undeserved love, they stand directly in line with Melanchthon and Luther and the entire witness of the Reformation. God's free mercy stands at the heart of our proclamation to this world, mercy that flows from God's two hands: the mercy of this beautiful creation and all of its bounty, on the one hand, and the mercy of Christ and of faith in him borne by the Holy Spirit, on the other.

Fourth, and finally, the Augsburg Confession confesses not simply faith alone but Christ alone. Now this is no "christo-monism," as if we were piously reducing God to Jesus. After all, "faith alone" clearly demands that the *Holy Spirit* work in us through Word and sacraments. Rather, Melanchthon was insisting that the heart and center of our relation to God came not from us or from our works but from Christ and his work *alone*. As the French Reformation scholar Marc Lienhard has written, Martin Luther was more than anything else a witness to Jesus Christ.[41] This stood at the center of his thought. Luther and Melanchthon both understood that, in a certain way, one could not *preach* faith. To do that was to turn faith back into a work. No, instead one had actually to preach the object of faith and its subject—that is, the One by whom and for whom faith came into being.

"We are forgiven for Christ's sake, who alone is the mediator to reconcile the Father," Melanchthon wrote in the German version of the Augsburg Confession, article 20. Christ is the One to whom faith clings; he is the One in whom human beings can trust. When this One appears to doubters in the upper room, when his voice is heard in the garden by the sobbing Mary Magdalene, then everyone else slips from view. Works dissolve and we cry, "Rabboni!" "My Lord and

41. Marc Lienhard, *Luther: Witness to Jesus Christ*, trans. Edwin H. Robertson (Minneapolis: Augsburg, 1982), especially his concluding chapter, pp. 371–94.

my God!" All of the ancient creeds too are simply variations on this single theme: "Christ alone!" After all, when the smoke clears (or the veil is lifted), who else is there whom we can trust? We have only the crucified and risen Savior.

Yet, like Melanchthon in article 20 (in which he announced that he was going to talk about faith and works and yet did not arrive at his intended subject until he was eighty percent through the article), this section has not yet touched on the connection of faith to ethics. The reason is clearly the same as the one Melanchthon gave: "Because at present the teaching concerning faith, which is the principal part of the Christian life, has not been emphasized for such a long time, as all must admit, but only a doctrine of works was preached everywhere."[42] All people who have the old creature around their necks (that is, all of us) have no clue about the grace and mercy of God in Christ. They have no clue about faith. They have been sold a mess of pious pottage in exchange for their glorious birthright as sons and daughters of God. For the indicative "You are forgiven," a statement one can trust, we have once again inserted the subjunctive "May God forgive you" or the jussive "God forgive you." Hearing such dissembling, sinners should shout, "Well, does God or not?" Once again, uncertainty rears its ugly head, and the law rules.

If pastors insist on uttering a word or two about the relation of faith and ethics in the parish, they should take to heart what Melanchthon wrote in article 20.

> Further, it is taught that good works should and must be done, not that a person relies on them to earn grace, but for God's sake and to God's praise. Faith alone always takes hold of grace and forgiveness of sin. Because the Holy Spirit is given through faith, the heart is also moved to do good works. [In the Latin version Melanchthon adds] For Ambrose [actually, Prosper of Aquitaine] says: "Faith is the mother of the good will and the righteous action." That is why this teaching concerning faith is not to be censured for prohibiting good works. On the contrary, it should be praised for teaching the performance of good works and for offering help as to how they may be done. For without faith and without Christ human nature and human power are much

42. CA XX.8 (German), in BC, 54.

too weak to do good works: such as to call on God, to have patience in suffering, to love the neighbor, to engage diligently in legitimate callings, to be obedient, to avoid evil lust, etc. Such lofty and genuine works cannot be done without the help of Christ, as he himself says in John 15: "Apart from me you can do nothing."[43]

Faith alone and Christ alone put all of human work in perspective, free believers from false perceptions concerning works, and allow them to serve their neighbor. The pastoral necessity of unburdening the conscience (*Gleichmut*) and the freedom to make moral decisions based on balance and fairness for that very conscience (*Gewissen*) find their origin for Christians in *Glaube*, faith in Christ alone.

Gemeinschaft: Community

Up to this point, some might imagine that Luther's ethics bordered on the individualistic and did not encourage Christians to think more holistically. In fact, Americans are the ones who think individualistically about Luther's ethics; Luther always thought in terms of the community—that is (in German), of the *Gemeinschaft*. Thus, this final category will disabuse all people born since the Enlightenment of the eighteenth century that one must think in individualized, personalistic terms.[44]

One of the best ways into Luther's thought on this matter came in some of his earliest comments on the Lord's Prayer, published in 1519.[45] It included a lengthy explanation of the introduction, "Our Father in heaven," concluding with these words:

> Finally, notice how carefully Christ organized this prayer. For he does not allow individuals to pray simply for themselves alone but for the entire assembly of all people. For he does not teach us to say, "My Father," but "Our Father." This prayer is spiritual community property.

43. CA XX.27–40, in BC, 56–57. To the Latin version, Melanchthon again adds a reference to the ancient church, this time to a hymn to the Holy Spirit: "And the church sings: 'Without your will divine / Naught is humankind / All innocence is gone.'"
44. This line of thought was first suggested to me at a pastors' conference in Nebraska. I am indebted to the unnamed questioner for pushing me on this very point.
45. WA 2:74–130 (=LW 42:15–81).

Thus, a person should deprive no one of it, not even enemies. For since he is the Father of us all, he desires that we ought to be brothers [and sisters] among ourselves, love one another dearly, and pray for each other just as for ourselves.[46]

Notice that even recognizing the communal nature of prayer had ethical consequences for Luther. Even enemies were included in the "our" of the "Our Father." Moreover, he called this a kind of spiritual community property, in a society that cherished its "commons"—land that belonged to all the people in a village or town. One might liken the Lord's Prayer today to a national treasure or a national park: something that belongs to everyone.

Another crucial discussion of the role of community occurs in the Large Catechism, where Luther set about to define *church*. He focused on one of the most obscure phrases in the Creed, "*communio sanctorum.*" Today, some scholars argue that the phrase could be better translated "participation in holy things" (that is, participation in the sacraments), since it comes at exactly the place where the Nicene Creed talks about baptism. Luther, however, had no way of anticipating this interpretation, although he did know that the phrase was a later addition to the Apostles' Creed. He also realized that a literal translation of the phrase into German made little sense—no more than it makes sense in English. He argued that *communio* should have been translated not "communion" but "community" (*Gemeinde*) and the entire phrase as "a holy community."[47] However, it was his remarkable paraphrase that provides a glimpse into the communal nature of Luther's thought.

I believe that there is on earth a holy little flock and community of pure saints under one head, Christ. It is called together by the Holy Spirit in one faith, mind, and understanding. It possesses a variety of gifts, and yet is united in love without sect or schism. Of this community I also am a part and member, a participant and co-partner in all the blessings it possesses. . . . Therefore everything in this Christian community is so ordered that everyone may daily obtain full forgiveness of

46. WA 2:86, 7–13 (=LW 42:26).
47. LC, Creed, 49, in BC, 437.

sins through the Word and signs appointed to comfort and encourage our consciences as long as we live on earth.[48]

He made this same connection between church and forgiveness in the Small Catechism, when he stated, "Daily in this Christian Church the Holy Spirit abundantly forgives all sins—mine and those of all believers in Christ."[49]

More than that, in the Large Catechism he summarized the entire third article this way:

> This, then, is the article that must always remain in force. For creation is now behind us, and redemption has also taken place, but the Holy Spirit continues his work without ceasing until the Last Day, and for this purpose he has appointed a community on earth, through which he speaks and does all his work. For he has not yet gathered together all of this Christian community, nor has he completed the granting of forgiveness. Therefore we believe in him who daily brings us into this community through the Word, and imparts, increases, and strengthens faith through the same Word and the forgiveness of sins.[50]

The verb in the Small Catechism that Luther applied only to the Holy Spirit's work in the church, "gathers," has a prominent place here. Gathering and forgiving were the chief communal works of the Holy Spirit through the Word, designed to create and increase faith throughout the whole church.

If these comments of Luther provided the underlying drumbeat of his communal ethic, then in addition he sounded a clear theme of this ethic in his Invocavit sermons of 1522, described above. His opening lines from the very first sermon were an interesting mixture of the individual with the communal.[51] Each of us must die on our own; we can yell into each other's ears, but we must all face death alone. For Luther, however, this meant that each person had to know for certain the basis of his or her salvation: first Christ alone, and second faith alone. The third point echoed a different, communal note.

48. LC, Creed, 51–52, 55, in BC, 437–38.
49. SC, Creed, 6, in BC, 356.
50. LC, Creed, 61–62, in BC, 439.
51. WA 10/3:1, 15–22 and 2, 16–18 (=LW 51:70).

Third, we must also have love and do to others through love as God has done for us through faith. Without this love faith is nothing. As St. Paul says in 1 Corinthians 13, "If I had the tongues of angels and could speak about faith in highest measure but had no love, so I am nothing." And here, dear friends, is there not a complete lack and no trace in any one of this love? Note very well that you have not been thankful to God for such a rich treasure and gift.[52]

That is to say, Luther gave them an A in doctrine but an F in love. He went on to point out that the weak are precisely the Christian community's concern, "lest Wittenberg become a Capernaum." You can teach any *Esel* (jackass) to recite the faith. But God's realm consists not in words but in power and deed. "In this case, dear friends, each person must not do what he or she has the right to do. Instead, they must give up their rights and see what is necessary and helpful for his or her brother or sister, as St. Paul did."[53]

Indeed, we have all kinds of examples in Luther and Melanchthon's lifetime that show how communally they regarded ethics, by which they intended not simply some sort of tyrannical majority rule but precisely preference for the weak. Moreover, the Reformers' behavior also made clear that there was no "Lone Ranger" theology operating in Wittenberg. Theologically and ethically, the Wittenberg faculty worked together. Testimony of these communal consultations were the countless memoranda, opinions, complaints, and ordination certificates signed by more than one person. Furthermore, the official opinions from Wittenberg often evinced a similar communal flavor. So Luther's ethics may be reduced to three simple words: *Gleichmut*, *Gewissen*, and *Glaube*, or, translated, *aequitas*, *conscientia*, and *fides*, or, translated again, reasonableness, weakness, and trust in Christ alone, all done in the context of Christian *Gemeinschaft*, *ecclesia*, or assembly.

52. WA 10/3:3, 5–9 and 4, 1–2 (=LW 51:71), translating the original notes and not the published version, on which LW 51 is based.
53. WA 10/3:5, 20–22 (=LW 51:71).

5

Example

Luther Interpreting Galatians 3:6–14

Over the course of his career Luther interpreted many parts of the Bible both in the lecture hall and from the pulpit.[1] Thus, already in the sixteenth century commentaries on (among other things) Genesis, Deuteronomy, some Psalms, the Minor Prophets, parts of the Gospels of Matthew and John, the Pastoral Epistles, 1 and 2 Peter and Jude, and Galatians appeared. In addition, manuscripts for his early lectures on the Psalms, Romans, Galatians, and Hebrews were preserved and published in the nineteenth and twentieth centuries. Indeed, of the original fifty-four-volume English translation of Luther's works, thirty are devoted to his exegetical work. If we include his commentaries on the appointed Sunday Gospel and Epistle texts for the standard one-year lectionary, called his *Church* and *House Postils*, Luther commented on at least a portion of almost every book in the New Testament.

1. This chapter is based on a presentation the author delivered at the "Paul's Letter to the Galatians & Christian Theology" conference at the University of St. Andrews, Scotland, in July 2012, and is scheduled to be published as part of its proceedings.

The history of biblical interpretation, as Gerhard Ebeling once proclaimed, defines the history of the church.[2] More art than science, it requires that one must first suspend disbelief and view a particular theologian's biblical interpretation as unique within its own setting. This implies taking care neither to impose one's own judgments about the text on some deceased saint of the church (who, after all, is dead and cannot defend him- or herself) nor, on the contrary, to let the deceased saint impose his or her judgments on us (à la: "Luther said it; I believe it; that settles it"). In the case of Martin Luther, practicing this art is all the more necessary, given his radical theology and hermeneutic as outlined in the previous chapters. This chapter focuses on Galatians—what Luther once referred to, using his wife's name, as his "Katie von Bora"—and gives us a chance to see how, at two different times in his career, Luther interpreted it. It will confirm many of the themes discussed in the previous chapters, but it will also demonstrate just how dynamic and surprising Luther's approach to the biblical message really is.

Regarding Paul's letter to the Galatians, Luther left posterity with four sources of interpretation:[3] an initial set of lectures from 1516 to 1517, a first published commentary of 1519 (heavily revised in 1523), a second set of lectures in 1531, and a commentary published in 1535.[4] This chapter provides a snapshot of the Reformer at work, as he struggled to make evangelical sense of Paul's comments in Galatians 3:6–14.

In recent years, an approach to the interpretation of Paul, called by its supporters the "New Perspective on Paul," has argued that Paul's central argument in Romans and Galatians has less to do with justification by faith and more with removing restrictions of Jewish law (especially circumcision) and with the acceptance of Gentiles within

2. Gerhard Ebeling, *Kirchengeschichte als Geschichte der Auslegung der Heiligen Schrift* (Tübingen: Mohr, 1947).

3. This is unlike Romans, where an early set of lectures (never meant for publication) and a widely popular preface to the book, written initially for his 1522 German translation of the New Testament, are all that we have from Luther on this book.

4. They are found, respectively, in WA 57/2:III–XXVI and 5–108; WA 2:436–618 (English translation of the commentary: LW 27:153–410); and WA 40/1–2 (combining the lectures and commentary [English translation of the commentary: LW 26 and LW 27:3–149]).

the nascent Jesus communities springing up throughout the Roman Empire.[5] Martin Luther in particular and Lutheran interpreters of Paul in general have been attacked as insensitive to the realities of first-century Judaism and its Christian offshoot. Careful examination of the history of biblical interpretation, however, reveals that this "new" school is actually a revival of an ancient approach to Paul that Martin Luther and Philip Melanchthon were familiar with and rejected, especially as defended by the famous Dutch humanist Erasmus of Rotterdam. Moreover, this rejection arose not out of theological hubris or the West's "introspective conscience" but out of specific exegetical convictions.[6]

The *Argumentum*

As noted in chapter 3, to appreciate fully the distinctive qualities of the contributions to biblical interpretation by Luther, one must never lose sight of the unique shape of Reformation commentaries. Unlike medieval ones, where dividing the text using rules of logic and resolving contradictions took center stage, Luther's published works and those by others from the Wittenberg school of biblical interpretation always began with an *argumentum*, a detailed outline of the biblical author's main argument. Luther's much more scholastic first lectures on Galatians of 1516–17 were still divided into medieval glosses and scholia and introduced Paul's main theme in a single sentence.[7]

Luther was not the first one to employ an opening *argumentum* in interpreting a text. Indeed, Renaissance interpreters discussed the

5. For a summary of this approach, see Erik Heen, "A Lutheran Response to the New Perspective on Paul," *Lutheran Quarterly* 24 (2010): 263–91, and the literature cited there.

6. Krister Stendahl, "The Apostle Paul and the Introspective Conscience of the West," *Harvard Theological Review* 56 (1963): 199–215; reprinted in Krister Stendahl, *Paul among Jews and Gentiles* (Philadelphia: Fortress, 1976), 78–96.

7. WA 57/2:5, 11–16: "In no other letter does [Paul] commend his apostolate with such effort and such a line of arguments as in this one, which, as he testifies, he wrote in his own hand. He did not do these things out of any pride but rather out of great necessity, so that the Gospel would not be subverted by those from the Jews who believed and taught the necessary observance of the law and so made them trust in works rather than in grace."

argumentum for all kinds of texts. They too believed that authors actually had a point to make when they wrote and that later readers could best understand what they were reading by paying attention to the author's central themes. Whether Luther succeeded in unlocking Paul's intent or not, he clearly began with the premise that, working with the best tools that sixteenth-century university training had to offer—grammar, rhetoric, and logic—and concentrating on the author's main point, an interpreter could best unlock what the apostle was trying to say. It is not such bad advice to follow today.

As common as this category was throughout the Renaissance, for Wittenberg's exegetes the *argumentum* was never trivial but had broad implications for Christian life and thought. As we have observed in the preceding chapters, Luther argued that although all biblical texts were truly God's Word, they were not necessarily God's Word for him or his immediate hearers. In the case of Paul's writings, however, it was Erasmus of Rotterdam, that mercurial humanist and supporter of Rome, who argued (on the basis of St. Jerome) that the first eleven chapters of Romans were only about Jewish law and had little or no application to the sixteenth-century reader. Wittenberg's exegetes fought tooth and nail against such irrelevancy by insisting that the terms *law*, *gospel*, *faith*, and *grace* had far wider application than simply a struggle over circumcision or other Jewish ceremonies.

Luther joined the battle not over Romans but over Galatians. Luther's approach to Galatians and its *argumentum* can only be understood in the light of his dismissal of Erasmian arguments to the contrary. This is not to say that Luther completely rejected Erasmus's annotations on and paraphrase of this book. Erasmus was the single-most-important biblical scholar of the early sixteenth century. Indeed, Luther's 1519 commentary is filled with praise for him. But these positive assessments revolved around the meaning of specific Greek texts. Moreover, in the second edition of 1523, almost every favorable reference to Erasmus disappeared.

We already can glean from Luther's correspondence just how disappointed Luther was with Erasmus and the patristic source (Jerome) on which he relied for his interpretation. On October 19, 1516, just as he commenced lecturing on Galatians, Luther wrote the following in a letter to his confidant Georg Spalatin, who oversaw the University of Wittenberg for the Saxon Elector:

> What disturbs me about that most erudite man, Erasmus, are these things, my dear Spalatin: that in his interpretation of the apostle [Paul] he understands the righteousness of works or of the law or one's own righteousness (for so the apostle calls it [in Romans 10:3]) as those ceremonial and figurative observations. Moreover, he does not want the apostle to speak plainly in Romans 5 about original sin (which at least he admits [exists]).[8]

After praising Augustine's contrasting approach and pointing out that many other church fathers agreed with Augustine, Luther returned to a comparison of his approach to that of Erasmus. "I do not at all doubt that in this I disagree with Erasmus, because in interpreting the Scriptures I simply esteem Jerome less than Augustine, while he esteems Augustine less than Jerome in everything."[9] Then, returning to the question of the law, he wrote,

> Therefore the righteousness of the law or of deeds is in no way only in ceremonies but more correctly also in the deeds of the entire Decalogue. When things are done outside of faith in Christ, although they make Doers, Rulers, and clearly upright men from a human perspective, nevertheless they do not taste more righteous than sour figs. For we do not, as Aristotle thinks, become righteous by doing righteous deeds—except in a counterfeit way—but righteous people (as I would say), by being made and being [righteous], do righteous deeds. First it is necessary for the person to be changed, then [come] works. Abel was pleasing [to God] before his offerings.[10]

Reading Luther's *argumenta* to Galatians from 1519 and 1535 makes clear that interpreting Paul's writings in the light of Jewish ceremonial law was not a new approach to the apostle and that Luther was fully aware of this alternative, rejecting it on not simply theological but also exegetical grounds. Indeed, the alternatives of a

8. WA Br 1:70, 4–8 (no. 27).
9. WA Br 1:70, 17–19.
10. WA Br 1:70, 25–32.

moralistic or legalistic interpretation of Paul, on the one hand, and an interpretation grounded in the unconditional mercy of God in Christ, on the other, have faced the church and its exegetes from the patristic period to the present. In present-day struggles to interpret not simply Galatians and Romans but also every text of Scripture, this debate continues.

How, then, did this rift between Erasmus and Luther reflect itself in Luther's introductions to his commentaries on Galatians? Here is the first sentence of Luther's *argumentum* from 1519:

> Although the Galatians had first been taught a sound faith by the apostle (that is, taught to trust in Jesus Christ alone, not in their own righteous [deeds] or in those of the Law), later on they were again misled by the false apostles into trusting works of legal righteousness; for they were very easily deceived by the fact that the name and the example of the great and true apostles were falsely appealed to as commending this.[11]

Luther cut short any attempt to reduce Paul's argument to one over Jewish ceremonies and insisted on contrasting human righteousness of law to the righteousness of faith in Christ. In 1535, Luther stated it this way in his *argumentum*:

> First of all, we must speak about the *argumentum*—that is, about the issue with which Paul deals in this epistle. This is the *argumentum*: Paul wants to establish the teaching of faith, grace and the forgiveness of sins, or Christian righteousness, so that we may have perfect knowledge of and grasp the difference between Christian righteousness and all other kinds of righteousness. For righteousness is of many kinds.[12]

Luther then defined political righteousness, the ceremonial righteousness found in papal and other traditions—all of which parents and teachers may pass down to the next generation, as long as they do not teach that they can forgive sin or placate God or merit grace. To this he added the legal righteousness of the Decalogue, which "we

11. WA 2:451, 2–5 (=LW 27:161, with corrections).
12. WA 40/1:40, 15–19 (=LW 26:4, with corrections).

teach after teaching about faith." He then contrasted these forms with Christian righteousness.

> Over and above all these there is the righteousness of faith or Christian righteousness, which is to be distinguished most carefully from all the others. For they are all contrary to this righteousness, both because they proceed from the laws of emperors, the traditions of the pope, and the commands of God and because they consist in our works and can be done by us either "from our own natural powers," as the sophists call it, or even from God's gift (for these kinds of righteousness of works are also God's gift, as are all of our possessions). But this most excellent righteousness (namely, of faith) which God imputes to us through Christ apart from our works, is neither political, nor ceremonial, nor the righteousness of the divine law, nor does it rest in our works but is quite the opposite. That is, this righteousness is a completely passive righteousness, just as those listed above are active. For here we do nothing and render nothing to God, but we only receive and suffer another—namely, God—to work in us. Therefore it is legitimate to call this righteousness of faith or Christian righteousness passive. And this righteousness, which the world does not understand, is hidden in mystery—indeed, Christians themselves do not sufficiently understand it and only with difficulty grasp it in the midst of assaults [*tentationes*; the Latin equivalent for Luther of *Anfechtungen*]. Therefore, it must always be hammered home and cultivated by continuous practice, and whoever does not grasp or take hold of it in afflictions and terrors of conscience cannot stand fast. For there is no other firm and certain consolation for consciences than this passive righteousness.[13]

Nearly twenty years after complaining about Erasmus's approach to Paul and the law in his letter to Spalatin, Luther continued to view Galatians in light of God's unconditional mercy in Christ alone and not as a discussion of Jewish ceremonies.

Galatians 3:6–14 in 1519

As we already saw in chapter 3, readers of the Bible make an egregious error when they neglect the author's main point. Then biblical

13. WA 40/1:40, 28–30 and 41, 12–26 (=LW 26:4–5, with corrections).

interpretation devolves into proof texting. Similarly, only in the context of Luther's definition of Paul's basic argument in Galatians can one appreciate his specific comments, in this case on Galatians 3:6–14. That text reads (in the NRSV translation):

> Just as Abraham "believed God, and it was reckoned to him as righteousness," so, you see, those who believe are the descendants of Abraham. And the scripture, foreseeing that God would justify the Gentiles by faith, declared the gospel beforehand to Abraham, saying, "All the Gentiles shall be blessed in you." For this reason, those who believe are blessed with Abraham who believed. For all who rely on the works of the law are under a curse; for it is written, "Cursed is everyone who does not observe and obey all the things written in the book of the law." Now it is evident that no one is justified before God by the law; for "The one who is righteous through faith will live."[14] But the law does not rest on faith; on the contrary, "Whoever does the works of the law will live by them." Christ redeemed us from the curse of the law by becoming a curse for us—for it is written, "Cursed is everyone who hangs on a tree"—in order that in Christ Jesus the blessing of Abraham might come to the Gentiles, so that we might receive the promise of the Spirit through faith.

In 1519, Luther's commentary still reflected the style and approach of late-medieval interpretation of Scripture. As a result, he did not discuss directly the overall structure of Paul's argument in chapter 3 as he would in 1535 but instead approached the verses individually. At the same time, he commented extensively on the patristic and later interpretations of the text, especially focusing on Jerome, whose Galatians commentary Erasmus followed closely.

Luther began chapter 3 by examining Jerome's two solutions to Paul's apparent harshness (in talking about the Galatians being bewitched). He rejected Jerome's argument that this reflected the Galatians' characteristics as easily bewitched, but he accepted Jerome's view that Paul treats the Galatians as children, given how they had moved from greater things of faith to lesser things by trusting the law again. In Galatians 3:3, Luther took issue with Jerome's interpretation and his distinction between works of the (ceremonial) law and good

---

14. Using the alternate reading in the NRSV.

works. Far from arguing that one received the Holy Spirit through good works as Jerome imagined, Luther insisted instead that the Holy Spirit came through preaching heard with faith. "The apostle is referring not only to Ceremonial Law but to absolutely every law; for since faith alone justifies and does good works, it follows that absolutely no works of any law whatever justify, nor are the works of any law good, only those of faith."[15] He then discussed at length the necessity of hearing God's Word with faith.

Through verse 5, then, Luther understood Paul discussing the experience of the Galatians. With verse 6 he then noted that Paul introduced the example of Abraham. Luther realized that Paul had abbreviated the discussion here, and he assumed that the Galatians were already familiar with the fuller arguments, which they had heard directly from Paul and which were explicated extensively in Romans 4. What jumps out at the reader in this part of Luther's exposition is his deep concern for what the Danish scholar Leif Grane discovered already in Luther's interpretation of Romans from 1515 to 1516—namely, the *modus loquendi theologicus*, the theological mode of speaking.[16] Here Luther addressed this issue from two angles. On the one hand, Luther noticed that Paul read Scripture in a peculiar way. On the other hand, Luther pointed out that Paul did not follow "the rules of logical arguments."[17] As we will see, it is this second point that demonstrates how Luther's theology of the cross plays itself out in his reading of the Bible.

On the first point, Luther stated, "From this passage you see how intently and observantly Paul wants Scripture to be read. For who would have drawn these proofs from the text of Genesis?"[18] Paul's approach to Scripture defied both Paul's own interlocutors, the pseudo-apostles, and also Luther himself, who was equally dumbfounded by Paul's arguments that Abraham's faith preceded the work of circumcision and that he did not earn the right to have Isaac as an heir but received it as a result of a "counter-promise" (*repromissio*) and thus through faith, which created all of Abraham's offspring.

15. WA 2:508, 12–15 (=LW 27:248, with corrections).
16. See Leif Grane, *Modus loquendi theologicus: Luthers Kampf um die Erneuerung der Theologie (1515–1518)* (Leiden: Brill, 1975).
17. WA 2:511, 11 (=LW 27:252).
18. WA 2:511, 1–2 (=LW 27:252, with corrections).

Second, Paul was also a poor logician. Now, at first blush this seems a rather nasty thing to say about an apostle. But Luther's approach here has to do with the intrinsic foolishness of the gospel itself. Only when interpreters take seriously the nonlogical arguments Paul and other biblical authors make can they unlock the true wisdom of God. Here is how Luther argued in 1519. He viewed Paul's argument in verses 5–7 as an abbreviated logical argument in which the minor premise is missing. The major premise was simply "Abraham's faith was reputed [or reckoned] as righteousness [v. 6]," and the conclusion "therefore receiving the Spirit and doing virtuous deeds is from the hearing of faith [v. 5]."[19] The missing "middle term" of the Pauline syllogism was that faith being reckoned for righteousness was identical to receiving the Spirit (v. 5). But Luther recognized a possible tautology: "Therefore, either [Paul] proves nothing or 'to receive the Spirit' and 'to be reckoned for righteousness' are the same thing."[20]

Another important aspect of Luther's reading of Scripture arose from his fierce insistence on discovering the precise meaning of biblical language. He rarely took for granted a Greek or Hebrew word's definition but used every tool at his disposal to unlock the specific intent behind an author's use of a particular word or phrase. In this section of his 1519 Galatians commentary we have a fine example reflecting this concern and how Luther over a period of three years changed his mind. In 1519 Luther obliquely questioned Erasmus's suggestion for translating *charis Theou* in Greek (generally translated in Luther's day and ours as "the grace of God") as "*favor Dei*" ("God's favor"). For now, he rejected the notion and stuck with the medieval notion that grace was an infused power or gift.

> Because [the preceding] is also true, therefore it is also repeated, lest divine reckoning be thought to be nothing outside God, considering that there are [those (namely, Erasmus)] for whom the word of the apostle, *gratia*, is thought to mean favor rather than gift. For when God favors and reckons, the Spirit truly is received—gift and grace.

19. WA 2:511, 12 (=LW 27:252). For details, see the St. Andrews lecture.
20. WA 2:511, 14–15 (=LW 27:252). Thus, the entire syllogism reads: major: (Abraham's) faith was reckoned for righteousness (v. 6); minor: faith to be reckoned as righteousness is the same as to receive the Spirit; conclusion: therefore faith receives the Spirit (v. 6).

Otherwise, if grace only signifies favor as favor is practiced among human beings, it was and remains in God from eternity. For as God loves in reality and not only in word, so also he favors in the present reality and not only in word.[21]

By 1521, however, in his tract *Against Latomus* Luther supported Erasmus's arguments fully, probably as a result of conversations with Philip Melanchthon (who started defining *charis* as "favor" the previous year). There Luther insisted on translating *charis* exclusively as "*favor Dei*."[22] Then, in the second edition of the Galatians commentary of 1523, he simply deleted this section altogether, another indication of Luther's change of heart. If nothing else, this shift from 1519 to 1523 demonstrates just how carefully Luther paid attention to the biblical text and its proper translation and how much he was willing to learn from Melanchthon and even Erasmus.

In 1519, however, Luther still was using a medieval understanding of grace as that which makes a person acceptable to God by infusing the soul with a disposition of love. Here Luther wanted to avoid dividing words from reality. Whenever God promises, God delivers. Thus, what Luther worried about was an understanding of God's grace that simply defined a characteristic of God verbally (something "in God") without any connection to the real life of faith ("the present reality"). Later he discovered that he could make the same point even more forcefully by accepting Erasmus's (and Melanchthon's) definition of the Greek. God's favor and mercy are never merely characteristics in God but always faith-creating and relational: they really do something to us.

Returning to Luther's "criticisms" of Paul's logic, Luther also noticed a second poor syllogism in Paul, this time in verses 6–7. The text, "Abraham believed, therefore those who are from faith are Abraham's sons," is illogical, since Paul's Jewish opponents could as easily say,

---

21. WA 2:511, 15–21 (=LW 27:252 and the German translation in StLA 8:1472).

22. WA 8:106, 1–28. See Rolf Schäfer, "Melanchthon's Interpretation of Romans 5:15: His Departure from the Augustinian Concept of Grace Compared to Luther's," in *Philip Melanchthon (1497–1560) and the Commentary*, ed. Timothy J. Wengert and M. Patrick Graham (Sheffield: Sheffield Academic Press, 1997), 79–104. For a comparison of Luther and Melanchthon's theologies, see Martin Greschat, *Melanchthon neben Luther: Studien zur Gestalt der Rechtfertigungslehre zwischen 1528 und 1537* (Witten: Luther Verlag, 1965), especially 80–109.

"Abraham was circumcised, therefore the circumcised are his sons." Here, Luther argued, the missing term is the begetting of Isaac, which took place in the flesh but from faith in God's promise (given that Abraham was incapable of begetting a child from the flesh on his own). "Thus, [Isaac] is the son not so much of Abraham but of the one believing the God who promises."[23]

Luther's rigorous insistence on Paul's weak arguments continued with verse 8. First—and this solved a problem that vexed Jerome—Luther glossed the phrase, "Scripture foreseeing," with the words, "That is, the Spirit in Scripture."[24] He then could dismiss Jerome's worry that the apostle quoted Scripture according to its sense and not its actual text. Instead, Luther wondered how Paul could use this verse from Genesis at all, since it referred to Genesis 12, while the promise of an offspring did not occur until Genesis 15. Jerome solved the problem by referring the text to Genesis 22, and, although Luther granted that this might be the case (so that Paul's use of "you" was simply an abbreviated form of "your offspring"), he concluded the discussion with a surprising dismissal of the entire issue: "It makes no difference which he said here."[25] Why? "Because these things were said to Abraham, not to any old person or to the flesh but to one who believes, obeys, is spiritual and another person altogether—in short, to one who holds the promise—therefore it follows that Scripture wants to teach us that there are no sons of Abraham except such who would be sons and seed of this [believing] Abraham."[26] Such freedom in interpretation prevents us from simply kowtowing to Luther's own interpretation and from assuming that there is only one "right way" to interpret a text. For Luther and other early Lutheran interpreters such as Melanchthon, the point was to keep the main point in mind. Variety in interpretive possibilities did not for Luther undermine the certainty of God's promises embedded within these texts, and *that* certainty was his goal in interpreting the Bible.

So far, Luther had reconstructed Paul's argument something like this: Abraham had a son according to faith in the promise alone; I

23. WA 2:511, 32–33 (=LW 27:253).
24. WA 2:512, 4–5 (=LW 27:253).
25. WA 2:512, 17 (=LW 27:254).
26. WA 2:512, 18–21 (=LW 27:254, with corrections).

am a son according to faith in the promise; therefore I am a son of Abraham from faith. However, he even realized that this argument could be attacked. Thus, in commenting on verse 9, he reconstructed an objection to Paul's argument as follows: "But some quibbler will still object, 'Such a line of argumentation does not stand up: "Abraham believes, therefore those who believe are his sons," because Abraham indeed merited son and seed through faith, but it does not hence follow that his sons ought to believe.'"[27] Otherwise, Luther went on to say, anything that Abraham possessed, including Canaan, would have to believe.

Luther solved this "logical flaw" by referring in the first instance to the simplemindedness of the Galatians (unlike the Romans), who simply needed to know that "they cannot be children of Abraham unless they are like him."[28] But Luther also knew that a deeper mystery lurked here—namely, that the truth of the premises in this argument rested in God's reliability. "Since, however, the divine promise and predestination cannot be false, with no difficulty the conclusion [of the syllogism] will also be infallible that all who have been promised are among the faithful, so that the faith of those promised stands not on the necessity of works and their faith but on the reliability of divine election."[29] Indeed, divine election for Luther was nothing other than God's unconditional promise—the only trustworthy thing upon which one might build, since neither works nor even faith were that reliable. For Luther, then, the reliability of Scripture rested squarely in God's electing promise alone. (Later attempts to make Scripture an infallible science book or law book have nothing to do with his argument.) This means, as we have seen in chapters 1–3, that for Luther what really matters in biblical interpretation is discovering God's sovereign, irrevocable promise to us and letting it loose on our ears and hearts.

At the heart of Luther's understanding of the *modus loquendi* of both Scripture and Paul's logic, then, beat his discovery of God's completely unconditional, trustworthy, and foolish promise. Without this promise, Paul seemed to misquote and misunderstand Scripture,

27. WA 2:512, 33–36 (=LW 27:254, with corrections).
28. WA 2:513, 3–4 (=LW 27:254–55).
29. WA 2:513, 6–9 (=LW 27:255, with corrections).

proffered only weak arguments to make his case, and forced the reader to interpret everything according to human standards—whether of works or faith. On the contrary, if Scripture simply revealed the divine decision to have mercy, then only Paul's illogic truly comprehended what was at stake—the Spirit's understanding of God's heart.

But Luther's search for Paul's foolishness was not over. By quoting Deuteronomy 27:26 in Galatians 3:10, Paul turned Moses on his head and again spoke absurdly. "Look at the apostle's astounding syllogism!"[30] Moses had cursed those who did *not* do what was in the law; Paul cursed those who performed works of the law. Some, like Festus Porcius (cf. Acts 26:24), could well call Paul insane! Luther resolved this objection by distinguishing between doing and fulfilling the law. "Whoever are outside faith may indeed perform the works of the law, but they do not fulfill the law."[31] If the one circumcised did not fulfill the whole law, then surely neither did anyone else doing any other work of the law. Thus, Moses placed all under a curse because no one fulfilled any part of the law and thus everyone needed a redeemer, Christ. Those who seemed to fulfill the law were merely pretending.

Luther was never content, however, to reduce Scripture to interesting historical and theological facts. Instead, for him meaning included allowing a text's interpretation to address his own situation. In this case, Luther went after those he called "my neutralists" (that is, those who distinguished good works from meritorious works and argued that sinners could do good works that fulfilled the law).[32] Paul, these opponents argued (with Jerome and Erasmus), was only speaking of ceremonial works, which brought death and a curse. Luther argued instead that the ceremonial law was not evil unless one trusted it; Paul was on the contrary speaking of all law. Then Luther took on Jerome by name. Jerome had cleaned up Paul's logic by adding the words *every* and *all* to the text. Yet this ceremonial narrowing of the text contradicted Galatians 3:13–14, since Christ did not simply redeem from the curse of the ceremonial law, given that the Gentiles were never under that law. "For, as I have said before, Christ accomplishes too little if he only freed us from circumcision, Sabbaths, clothing,

30. WA 2:513, 23–24 (=LW 27:255).
31. WA 2:513, 32–33 (=LW 27:256).
32. WA 2:514, 7 (cf. 2:503, 7 and WA 5:408, 22).

foods, and ablutions and not from the far more serious sins against the law: lust, greed, wrath, ungodliness."[33] Jerome's argument turned Christ into a savior of bodies, not souls. Luther concluded: "But therefore the work of any law whatsoever is a sin and curse, if it is done outside of faith—that is, outside the purity of heart, innocence, and righteousness."[34] For Luther, what was written in the law was faith, and "this [faith] alone performs all things of the law."[35]

Following this line of argument, Luther then interpreted verse 11 as the underlying assumption for why Paul had cited Deuteronomy. He paraphrased Paul to say, "You hear from Moses that that one is cursed who does not do what has been written [in the law], and I at the same time have assumed that such are those who live from works."[36] Performing works of the law and keeping the law were, in Luther's view of Paul, two separate things. The keeping of the law occurred only by faith, as Paul's citation of Habakkuk 2:4 proved. Without faith the works of the law are death and unrighteous and thus do not "fulfill what is written" (cf. Deut. 27:26).

Luther then turned to verse 12, which he viewed as again reiterating Paul's main point that the law and faith are not the same. "Neither [the law] itself nor its works are from faith or with faith."[37] For Luther, Paul's citation of Leviticus 18:5 showed that the doers of law lived, but only in those deeds that evaded punishment and acquired the law's rewards; they did not live in God or as an offspring of believing Abraham but rather were dead toward God. Luther distinguished between outward appearances (where a human being seemed in the eyes of others to fulfill the law) and inward unrighteousness lived without faith, and he again attacked Jerome's interpretation, blaming it on the latter's false understanding of law and excessive allegorizing of the law learned from Origen. Far from the persons of the Old Testament being mere shadows and thus placing them under Moses' curse, Luther insisted that this "is altogether false, for

33. WA 2:514, 18–21 (=LW 27:257, with corrections).
34. WA 2:514, 22–24 (=LW 27:257, with corrections).
35. WA 2:514, 36 (=LW 27:257).
36. WA 2:514, 39–40 and 515, 1 (=LW 27:258, translating *sunt* as "rely on," and StLA 8:1475, translating *sunt* as "*umgehen*").
37. WA 2:515, 13–14 (=LW 27:258).

they lived before God justified and sanctified by faith, even before the law and the works of the law were commanded."[38] As we saw in chapter 1, for Luther faith alone unified the two Testaments, making everything and everybody revolve around faith in God's promised mercy in Christ.

This brings us, finally, to Luther's 1519 interpretation of verses 13–14 and Luther's understanding of salvation in Christ. In the first place, Luther's reading of Paul placed everyone under the curse of the law. As a result, from the outset he attacked late-medieval theologians who thought sinners could fulfill the law at least "according to the substance of the act" although not "according to the intention of the Law-Giver" (namely, God, who expected people to possess the habit of love first). Luther dismissed such an approach. "I find fault with those who are neither under the curse of the law nor require Christ, the redeemer."[39] Here the cause of the Reformation and Luther's interpretation of Paul converged. By trying to find a way out from under the curse through "doing what is in you," Luther's contemporaries had in his view eliminated Christ as redeemer.[40]

In contradistinction to such arguments, Luther insisted that those outside grace were sinning not by refraining from committing adultery or murder but by inward sins of lust, hatred, and the like. "For this hidden uncleanness of heart and flesh is not removed except by faith through Christ's grace."[41] The law's intent, he continued, was not that it be kept by earning grace but rather that it be kept but only with grace. Thus, the law forced a person to seek grace outside him or herself. "Therefore we who are without faith's grace are all under the law's curse."[42] This insight—that the law was supposed to drive a person to Christ and to grace, so that he or she could be stripped of works and merit and have only faith—drove Luther's entire approach to the law in Paul. "For since 'the righteous person lives' only 'by faith,' the curse of the law is clearly on unbelievers, lest we make

---

38. WA 2:515, 31–33 (=LW 27:259, with corrections). In the same section, Luther tried to rescue Jerome's approach, since later in the commentary Jerome admitted that all were also sinners according to the moral law.

39. WA 2:516, 9–10 (=LW 27:259, with corrections).

40. WA 2:516, 12 (=LW 27:260).

41. WA 2:516, 18–19 (=LW 27:260, with corrections).

42. WA 2:516, 21–22 (=LW 27:260, with corrections).

Christ's redemption worthless or only refer it to ceremonial things, from which even a human being could redeem us."[43]

In the same section, Luther linked these verses to Paul's comment in 2 Corinthians 5:21 ("God made Christ to be sin for us . . ."). Then, building on Paul's paradoxes in these two texts, Luther invented more "happy exchanges" of his own. "In an entirely similar turn of phrase, 'he died so that we may be life in him'; 'he was ashamed so that we might be made a boast in him'; 'he was made all things for us so that we might become all things in him.' That is, if we believe in him, then the law is already fulfilled and we are freed from the curse of the law."[44] For Luther, then, Paul's paradoxes of blessing and curse or of sin and righteousness were not texts to be explained away but manners of speaking that apply everywhere through faith.

Luther then mocked Jerome for trying to avoid admitting that Christ was cursed by God. For Luther, Jerome's objections missed Paul's point, which Jesus also affirmed by applying Isaiah 53:12 ("He was numbered with the transgressors") to himself. Luther linked Paul's argument (that the blessing comes to the Gentiles) to one of his key insights into Christian life: good works do not make people good, but good people do good works. Or, as he opined, "The Gentiles will be Abraham's sons, not because they imitate him but because they were given a promise. Therefore, they would also imitate him because they had become sons as a result of God's promising and fulfilling not as a result of their doing and imitating. For imitation does not make sons, but sonship makes imitators."[45]

Galatians 3:6–14 in 1535

In his book on Luther's second commentary on Galatians, Kenneth Hagen argues that Luther's exegetical method had more in common with a monastic reading of texts than with either scholastic or humanist approaches.[46] While this certainly helps to explain the length of

43. WA 2:516, 22–25 (=LW 27:260, with corrections).
44. WA 2:516, 33–36 (=LW 27:260, with corrections).
45. WA 2:518, 13–16 (=LW 27:260, with corrections).
46. Kenneth Hagen, *Luther's Approach to Scripture as Seen in His "Commentaries" on Galatians, 1519–1538* (Tübingen: Mohr Siebeck, 1993).

Luther's comments and the meditative form that they took, Hagen's theory is simply too narrow. At this point in his career, Luther employed all of the methods and approaches available to him to unlock the meaning of biblical texts. Thus, as we have already seen, his lectures and commentary featured a detailed *argumentum*, characteristic of humanist approaches to Scripture. He also referred to the Greek text, ancient commentaries, and the rhetorical turns in Paul's argument, which also had little to do with monastic readings of texts but much to do with the peculiar brand of Wittenberg humanism that marked all of its biblical exegesis. His expansive commentary of 1535, while certainly having much in common with a form of monastic *lectio divina*, does not finally fit into any one category cleanly, since Luther employed not only meditation per se (which was marked by conversation between the soul [or exegete] and God) but also paraphrase (a beloved humanist exegetical technique) and direct application of the text to Luther's own situation.[47] Luther's method evinces rather a homiletic style that assumed interpretation of individual verses only reached its goal when strengthening the hearers' faith.

In the 1535 commentary, Luther divided up Paul's arguments more clearly than in 1519, noting that the apostle began with an argument from experience (3:1–5) before moving on to an argument from Scripture, specifically Abraham (3:6–14), and finally to one based on a human analogy (3:15–18). Whereas in the first section of this chapter he again explicitly rejected reducing Paul's understanding of law to ceremonies, in the middle section, which is our interest here, he also had other, bigger fish to fry.

To appreciate Luther's approach, however, we need to identify some of his other exegetical techniques. In addition to the *argumentum*, described above, Luther especially used paraphrase and direct application to his current situation. These techniques arose out of his central theological commitment to the *modus loquendi* described above or, in the context of this commentary, better described as the *viva vox evangelii*—the living voice of the gospel. It represented Luther's struggle with the text of Paul as authority—that is, as a text that (to

---

47. See Mark U. Edwards, *Luther and the False Brethren* (Stanford, CA: Stanford University Press, 1975), and Timothy J. Wengert, "Luther and Melanchthon— Melanchthon and Luther." *Luther-Jahrbuch* 66 (1999): 55–88.

play on the original meaning of the Latin *auctoritas* [something au-
thored or produced]) produced something in the reader. For Luther,
as we saw in chapter 2, this "production" meant being condemned
and put to death through the law and being forgiven and brought to
life through the gospel.

Moreover, Luther employed paraphrase as an especially adept form
of such "authorization," since it allowed Paul to speak directly to the
sixteenth-century hearers or readers and with a fullness that brought
the apostle's words into their present situation. Luther intended to
bring lively meaning to Paul's words. Of the many examples in this
section of the commentary, consider Luther's remarks on Galatians
3:9 ("Therefore, those who are from faith will be blessed with faithful
Abraham").[48] Luther stated:

> Here the emphasis and whole force is in the word, "with *faithful* Abra-
> ham." For Paul is obviously distinguishing Abraham from Abraham by
> making one and the same person into two persons, as if he were saying:
> "There is an Abraham who does works and an Abraham who believes.
> We are not concerning ourselves with the Abraham who does works.
> For 'if he is justified by works, he has something to boast about, but
> not in the sight of God' [Rom. 4:2]. Let that begetting Abraham, who
> does works, who is circumcised and who observes the Law, properly
> apply to the Jews. But another Abraham applies to us—namely, the
> faithful one, the one of whom Scripture declares that through his
> faith he received the blessing of righteousness and that he received
> the promise of the same blessing for all those who believe as he did.
> As a result, the world is promised to Abraham, but as the one who
> believes. Therefore the whole world should be blessed (that is, should
> receive the imputation of righteousness) if it believed as Abraham."[49]

Luther simply explained the centrality of the phrase (in the Vulgate
translation that he followed) *"faithful* Abraham." He then used Paul's
parallel discussion of Abraham in Romans 4 to prove that the distinction of the two Abrahams came from Paul. (Indeed, as in 1519, throughout this section he referred to Paul's broader arguments in Romans.)

48. This represented the Latin Vulgate. Erasmus, on the basis of the Greek, translated
"are blessed." The German Bible followed the Greek as well (*"warden . . . gesegnet"*).
49. WA 40/1:386, 15–25 (=LW 26:244–45, with corrections), emphasis added.

Luther then investigated the meaning of the verb *to bless*. "The blessing is nothing other than the promise of the gospel," he began.[50] Being blessed meant to hear this very promise. "This promise is preached and spread through the gospel unto all nations."[51] The Hebrew prophets derived all of their prophecies from this blessing—spiritually understood. "In sum, all prophecies about Christ's reign and the spreading of the gospel into the entire world come from this text."[52] Luther viewed Paul's argument as a kind of analogy. Thus he wrote: "As the imputation of righteousness reached Abraham through the hearing of faith, so also it reached and now reaches all nations." Why could he say this? "For it is the voice [*sermo*] of the same God, which was first addressed to Abraham and afterwards to all nations."[53]

By shifting the promise of Abraham to all nations, Luther could apply the text to his own hearers and readers. "Therefore, 'to bless' is to preach and teach the word of the gospel, to confess Christ, and to spread knowledge of him to others." This was the priestly office continued in the New Testament "by preaching, by administering the sacraments, by absolving, by consoling, and by explaining the word of grace which Abraham had and which was his blessing. When he believed it, he received a blessing, so also we who believe it are blessed."[54]

What Luther saw Paul doing in interpreting Abraham's promise was what he also observed in the prophets—and what he thought he was doing: a dynamic reorientation of the original promise to a new set of hearers. "[The prophets] did not view the promises made to the fathers lifelessly [*frigide*], as did the impious Jews and as do the sophists and sectarians today, but they read and honed them with the greatest diligence and whatever they prophesied concerning Christ and his reign they drew from this source."[55] Here Luther grounded how he read Paul in how Paul and the prophets read Genesis: not "lifelessly" (that is, literally, as if the only point was to promise some

50. WA 40/1:386, 26 (=LW 26:245).
51. WA 40/1:386, 28–29 (=LW 26:245).
52. WA 40/1:387, 13–14 (=LW 26:245).
53. WA 40/1:387, 17–20 (=LW 26:245).
54. WA 40/1:387, 24–27 (=LW 26:245).
55. WA 40/1:387, 31–32 and 388, 12–13 (=LW 26:246).

land to Abraham) but spiritually, which was the only kind of blessing that can be received by faith.

If in the preceding Luther had hinted at the connection between Paul's description of Abraham's faith and his own day, he came right out and said so in the next lines. Here Luther used an "as then . . . so now" construction to make his point. "However, just as the Jews gloried only in the Abraham who does works, so the pope only proposes a Christ who does works or as an example."[56] Note that Luther's quarrel was not simply with a faulty interpretation of Abraham by some people in the past but with the analogous ways that people in his day misinterpreted both Abraham and Christ. In the 1530s, Wittenberg's theologians and supporters of Rome were fighting over whether Jesus' command to love one another was law or gospel.

> [The Pope] says, "Whoever wants to live in a godly way ought to walk as Christ walked, according to that passage in John 13[:15], 'I give to you an example, that as I did, you also should do.'" We do not deny that Christ's example is to be imitated by the godly and must be carefully followed, but through this example they do not become righteous before God. Paul here is introducing not a discussion about what we ought to do but on what grounds we are justified. Here Christ alone, dying for our sins and rising for our righteousness, must be set forth as our righteousness. Moreover, he must be apprehended by faith as gift not as example.[57]

Again Luther distinguished between the Abraham who worked and the Abraham who believed. "Thus the Abraham who had faith must be separated from the Abraham who did works as far as heaven is separated from earth. The one who has faith is a completely divine man, a son of God, the inheritor of the entire world, victor over the world, sin, death, the devil, etc. and thus who cannot be praised enough."[58] Thus, faith sufficed before God, while works and examples were for this world and the neighbor.

Luther introduced the next section (vv. 10–14) by pointing out that from the words "they will be blessed" Paul constructed an argument

56. WA 40/1:389, 12–13 (=LW 26:246).
57. WA 40/1:389, 13–20 (=LW 26:246–47).
58. WA 40/1:390, 21–24 (=LW 26:247).

from contraries. This exegetical insight was a crucial one for Luther. "For Scripture is filled with antitheses. It belongs to a clever person to discern the antitheses in the Scriptures and through them to be enabled to interpret the Scriptures."[59] Indeed, Luther found the key to interpreting Scripture precisely here, because such antitheses overturned reason and drove the reader to faith in Christ.

Paul and Luther both moved effortlessly—or, rather, paradoxically—from blessing to curse. Since the blessing was only found in the promise to Abraham as revealed in the gospel, anything outside that blessing was under a curse. To get out from under the curse of the law—both the divine law given to Moses and any other human laws and traditions—a person only had the promise of blessing or the faith of Abraham. In light of this, Luther introduced yet another wrinkle in his exegetical method, one that (as we saw in chapter 2) marked all Wittenberg exegetes: his insistence that part of the meaning of the text was wrapped up in its effect on the hearer. "It is extremely valuable to know this, because it avails for consoling consciences."[60]

Luther then picked up another important thread in Wittenberg exegesis, the distinction between faith's righteousness and civil or fleshly righteousness. He complained that Jerome and others ignored this distinction and thus confused what Paul was saying about the law spiritually with civil righteousness. Thus, although civil righteousness lay outside of Christ and faith, it was not ipso facto under a curse but simply did not serve divine righteousness. Only when one confused the two forms of righteousness did one come under the law's curse. Why did Luther make this distinction? His Roman opponents consistently argued that his position fomented rebellion.

> The pope and the bishops cannot stand this, but it is not fitting for us to keep silence. For we ought to confess the truth and say that the papacy is cursed, the laws and statutes of the emperor are cursed, because according to Paul whatever is outside the promise and faith of Abraham is cursed. When our adversaries hear this, they interpret our words perversely, as if we teach that the government is not to

59. WA 40/1:391, 17–19 (=LW 26:248).
60. WA 40/1:392, 19 (=LW 26:249). This phrase was not as clearly expressed in Luther's lectures (WA 40/1:392, 6).

be treated with respect but rather as if we were fomenting rebellion against the emperor.[61]

Against these charges, Luther insisted on distinguishing physical and spiritual blessings. Here we can see how attacks by his theological opponents, whose views he took very seriously, influenced what he said in his commentary. He heightened what he saw as a paradoxical, blanket statement in order to answer his own accusers.

> In sum, we say that all things are God's good creatures . . . ; that is, they are temporal blessings pertaining to this life. But the self-righteous of all ages—Jews, Papists, sectarians, etc.—confuse and mix together these things, because they do not distinguish between spiritual and corporal blessings. Thus they say, "We have the law, which is good, holy, and just. Therefore we are justified through it."[62]

Some things in Luther's interpretation of Galatians did not change. Just as in 1519 he saw the scandal of Paul's argument in verse 10—proving an affirmative statement from a negative one—so here too he called this "an amazing [*mirabilis*] proof,"[63] rather like proving from Jesus' statement in Matthew 19:17 ("If you observe the commandments of God, you will enter life") the very opposite ("If you do not observe the commandments, you will enter life"). "No one understands this text except by rightly holding the article of justification. Jerome sweats over this enough, but he never really explains it."[64] Luther, by contrast, never saw a contradiction in Scripture he did not like. So he created, then, a delightful absurdity: "If you have fulfilled the Law, you have not fulfilled it; if you have not fulfilled it, you have fulfilled it."[65] For Luther, it all came down to the verb *to do* (as in the one who *does* the law). Keeping the law, he argued, was not simply a matter of doing what was commanded but was instead a matter of the heart and thus keeping it *completely*. The very claim to be keeping the law meant relying on one's own works and hence, by that very reliance,

61. WA 40/1:394, 17–22 (=LW 26:250).
62. WA 40/1:395, 15–21 (=LW 26:250–51).
63. WA 40/1:396, 31 (=LW 26:252).
64. WA 40/1:397, 18–20 (=LW 26:252).
65. WA 40/1:397, 31 (=LW 26:252).

trusting in oneself and not in God, thus breaking the first commandments about God and hence all of the commandments. For him the
verb *to do* included faith. "Therefore, clearly and properly defined,
'to do' is simply to believe in Jesus Christ and, since the Holy Spirit
is received through faith in Christ, to do the things in the law."[66] He
then reverted to a favorite image for the relation between works and
faith, one that attacked the Aristotelian ethics he grew up with, where
a person became good by doing good. "Faith takes 'doers' themselves
and makes them into [good] trees, so that their deeds become fruit.
First there must be a tree, then the fruit. For apples do not make a
tree, but a tree makes apples. So faith first makes the person who
afterwards performs works."[67]

For Luther, the paradoxical nature of Paul's writing and, hence, of
the Word of God was never far from his mind. He found already in
verse 6 an impossible juxtaposition of "faith" and "righteousness."
Luther's "theology of the cross," which we examined in chapter 3,
provided the key for how God acts with sinners. In the case of Paul's
use of Abraham, it was patently absurd to reason that Abraham could
be justified by faith and not works. Luther began by defining faith as
radically as possible.

> Paul makes out of faith in God the supreme worship, the supreme
> submission, the supreme obedience and sacrifice. . . . To attribute glory
> to God is to believe in him, regard him as truthful, wise, righteous,
> merciful, and almighty, in short, to acknowledge him as the Author
> and Donor of every good. Reason does not do this, but faith does. It
> consummates the Deity; and, if I may put it this way, it is the creator
> of the Deity, not in God's substance but in us.[68]

Luther mentioned reason as the counterpoint to faith and, to
set up his argument, defined faith in terms of righteousness. Here
Luther used reason's definition of righteousness for his own ends.
Aristotle, Cicero, Justinian, and a host of other ancient authors
had defined *iustitia* as "giving to each his [or her] own." So Luther

66. WA 40/1:401, 20–22 (=LW 26:255).
67. WA 40/1:402, 13–17 (=LW 26:255).
68. WA 40/1:360, 17–18, 20–25 (=LW 26:226–27).

then defined faith as justifying "because it renders to God what is due to him."[69] In this case specifically, however, it meant admitting that what God speaks is true. The trouble, Luther explained, was that according to reason God speaks "impossible, mendacious, foolish, weak, absurd, abominable, heretical, and diabolical things."[70] Whether one was talking about Christ's presence in the Lord's Supper, baptism as regenerative, or the incarnation and crucifixion, all were completely absurd and unreasonable. Reason imagined that its own choices and works, rather than hearing and believing God's voice, pleased God.

As a result, reason had to die. "But faith slaughters reason and kills the beast that the whole world and all creatures cannot kill."[71] The notion that reason had to die related directly to Luther's understanding of the function of the law à la Paul ("I through the law died to the law," Gal. 2:19). Here the scandal of faith that "lets God be God"[72] destroyed the very claims of reason to freedom of choice and the power of its own works. "Thus, all upright people, entering with Abraham into the darkness of faith, kill reason, saying: 'Reason, you are foolish. You do not understand the things that belong to God. . . . Do not judge; but listen to the Word of God and believe it.'"[73]

As a consequence of this line of thinking, Luther defined faith and imputation: "For Christian righteousness consists in two things: faith in the heart and the imputation of God." Here, using scholastic terminology borrowed from Aristotle, he defined faith as formal righteousness. Rather than approve the medieval scholastic understanding of justification at this point, however, Luther did the opposite. Supported by Aristotelian logic, medieval theologians insisted that everything consisted of matter and form. For them faith was always *formed* by love.[74] Faith itself could only provide the material

69. WA 40/1:361, 12–14 (=LW 26:227). He made a similar move in his preface to Romans (WA DB 7:10, 28–33 and 11, 28–34).

70. WA 40/1:361, 15–16 (=LW 26:227).

71. WA 40/1:362, 15–16 (=LW 26:228).

72. Philip Watson, *Let God Be God! An Interpretation of the Theology of Martin Luther* (Philadelphia: Muhlenberg, 1950).

73. WA 40/1:362, 23–26 (=LW 26:228).

74. Here Jerome's Latin translation in the Vulgate rendered the Greek of Gal. 5:6 "faith formed by love" as opposed to "faith working through love."

component—giving what we might call the building blocks of faith (the facts or tenets of faith) rather than a completed faith formed by love.[75] Luther, on the contrary, insisted that faith itself without works of love was one's "formal" righteousness. There was no need of works of love or a habit of charity to complete it. Instead, whatever was lacking in faith—now understood as trust in God (giving God due honor)—was made up for in the divine imputation of Christ's righteousness, where both were gifts from God, not human works.

For Luther, then, proper interpretation of Paul revolved around proper definition of the words, which only happened in the midst of a struggle against reason, which "reasonably" imagined that Paul could not mean what he said but had to allow room for works. Luther's summary of Galatians 3:6 further confirmed that faithful interpretation revolved around such definition. "I have said these things to interpret the verse, 'And it was reckoned to him as righteousness,' in order that the students of Sacred Scriptures may understand how Christian righteousness is to be defined properly and accurately. . . . Here must [now] be added these specifics as *differentia*."[76] Luther used a line from Aristotle's *Analytics* to continue his definition by looking at *differentia*—that is, the genus and species of a thing.[77] In this case, Luther insisted that *iustitia* was composed of two parts: faith in the heart and God's reckoning of faith as perfect righteousness, the very mix he found in Paul's text, which combined faith and imputation. For Luther, only preserving this distinction led to understanding Paul properly.[78] Faith weakly attributed glory to God; God shored up this God-given faith with Christ's righteousness.

Precisely in this situation "is the Christian person at the same time [*simul*] righteous and sinner, holy and profane, an enemy and son of God." "The sophists," as Luther called them, did not believe this and so their teaching on justification only drove people to despair. "We, on the contrary, teach in the way described above, and we console the afflicted sinner."[79] This *simul* meant for Luther that the Christian, like

75. See, for example, Luther's criticism of this term in WA 40/1:225, 23–230, 28.
76. WA 40/1:366, 22–27 (=LW 26:231).
77. Cf. CR 13:521.
78. WA 40/1:368, 15–25 (=LW 26:232).
79. WA 40/1:368 (=LW 26:232–33).

the high priest, offered sacrifices morning and evening: in the evening slaying reason and in the morning glorifying God.

Luther's exposition of this section of Galatians culminated in a lengthy interpretation of verses 13–14. Here, all of the criticisms of past exegesis and of his contemporary opponents came to a head. The text itself comprised the very kind of outrageous, paradoxical language typical of Luther's theology of the cross. As Luther mentioned already in 1519, Jerome (followed by Erasmus) could not imagine how Christ could be cursed. Paul, of course, had quoted the Hebrew text incorrectly, so Jerome went about correcting Paul on that basis. But Luther found in such tinkering with Paul a remarkable irony: that Jerome and his opponents were willing to argue against the clear text of Paul in order to accommodate their own theological tastes, even if their motive was to shield pious souls from hearing that Christ was cursed. Rather than harmonize Paul with Deuteronomy, Luther preferred to let each text stand on its own. For Luther, that Christ became a curse *for us* was the highest doctrine and comfort Scripture could give the sinner, the dying, and those oppressed.

To prosecute his case and heighten the paradox, Luther employed a host of remarkable rhetorical ploys, quite foreign to modern expectations for good biblical commentary. But then, were Luther correct—namely, that this text from Paul claimed so central a place in the believer's heart—anything less challenging and personal would result in not taking Paul seriously at all. One of the ways Luther accomplished this was through what might be termed exegetical fantasy. The various concepts in the text—law, curse, Christ—received a voice as Luther reenacted the meaning of the text for his hearers and readers. Here his imaginative, homiletical method of interpretation took full flight, fueled by Paul's own powerful language. As a first attempt at explaining this verse, Luther simply stated,

> And all the prophets saw this, that Christ was to become the greatest thief, murderer, adulterer, robber, desecrator, blasphemer, etc., there has ever been anywhere in the world. He is not acting in his own person now. Now he is not the Son of God, born of the Virgin. But he is a sinner, who has and bears the sin of Paul, the former blasphemer, persecutor, and assaulter; of Peter, who denied Christ; of David, who

was an adulterer and a murderer. . . . In short, he has and bears all the sins of all people in his body.[80]

Here Luther used two of his favorite rhetorical techniques—congeries and examples—to interpret the text. A bit later on, he emphasized both the text's comfort and the "sophists'" betrayal of sinners by their interpretations. "This knowledge of Christ and most delightful comfort, that Christ became a curse for us to set us free from the curse of the law—of this the sophists deprive us when they segregate Christ from sins and from sinners and set him only before us as an example to be imitated."[81]

For Luther, Christ becoming a curse for us equated to his incarnate existence. Suddenly, the readers' own reasonable objections were given a voice. "But it is highly absurd and insulting to call the Son of God a sinner and a curse!" he stated, but then continued, "If you want to deny that he is a sinner and a curse, then deny also that he suffered, was crucified, and died."[82] By insisting on "faith formed by love" as the way to remove sin, the "papists" had taken all power from the incarnation itself. "This is clearly to unwrap Christ and to unclothe him from our sins, to make him innocent, to burden and overwhelm ourselves with our own sins, and to behold them, not in Christ, but in ourselves. This is to abolish Christ and make him useless."[83]

With this, Luther set the stage for a dramatic approach to interpreting this text.

> This is the most joyous of all doctrines and the one that contains the most comfort. It teaches that we have the indescribable and inestimable mercy and love of God. For when the merciful Father saw that we were being oppressed and held under a curse through the Law, and that we could not be liberated from it by anything, he sent his Son into the world, heaped all the sins of all people upon him, and said to him: "Be Peter the denier; Paul the persecutor, blasphemer, and assaulter; David the adulterer; the sinner who ate the apple in paradise; that thief on

80. WA 40/1:433, 26–32 (=LW 26:277).
81. WA 40/1:434, 21–24 (=LW 26:278). Luther equated the text to 2 Cor. 5:21 and John 1:29.
82. WA 40/1:434, 29–36 (=LW 26:278).
83. WA 40/1:436, 27–31 (=LW 26:279).

the cross. In short, be the person of all human beings, the one who has committed the sins of all people. And thus see to it that you pay and make satisfaction for them." Then the law comes and says: "I find him a sinner, who takes upon himself the sins of all people. I do not see any other sins than those in him. Therefore let him die on the cross!" And so it attacks him and kills him. By this deed the whole world is purged and expiated from all sins and thus also set free from death and from all evil. But when sin and death have been abolished by this one man, God would not see anything in the whole world, especially if it were to believe, other than sheer cleansing and righteousness. And if any remnants of sin were to remain, still for the sake of Christ, the shining Sun, God would not notice them.[84]

Of course, here Luther used not only drama but also the metaphor of Christ "satisfying" humanity's debt of sin. Yet scarcely a page later Luther employed a very different, battle-like picture for the effect of Christ taking the curse upon himself.

Now let us see how two such extremely contrary things come together in this person. Not only my sins and yours but the sins of the entire world—past, present, and future—attack him, try to damn him, and do in fact damn him. But because in that same person, who is the highest, the greatest, and the only sinner, there is also eternal and invincible righteousness, therefore these two converge: the highest, the greatest, and the only sin; and the highest, the greatest, and the only righteousness. Here one of them of necessity must yield and be conquered, since they come together and collide with tremendous force. Thus the sin of the entire world attacks righteousness with the greatest possible impact and fury. What happens? Righteousness is eternal, immortal, and invincible. Sin too is a most powerful and cruel tyrant, dominating and ruling over the whole world, capturing and placing all people in captivity. In short, sin is the greatest and most powerful god who devours the whole human race. . . . He, I say, attacks Christ and wants to devour him as he has devoured all the rest. But he does not see that he is a person of invincible and eternal righteousness. In this duel, therefore, it is necessary for sin to be conquered and killed, and for righteousness to prevail and live. Thus in Christ all sin is conquered, killed, and buried; and righteousness remains the victor and the ruler

84. WA 40/1:437, 18–27 and 238, 12–18 (=LW 26:280).

eternally. Thus also death, which is the almighty empress of the entire world . . . clashes against life with full force and is about to conquer it and swallow it; and what it attempts, it accomplishes. But because life was immortal it emerged victorious when it had been conquered, conquering and killing death in turn. . . . Thus the curse, which is divine wrath against the whole world, has the same conflict with the blessing—that is, with the eternal grace and mercy of God in Christ.[85]

The final thing to note about Luther's interpretation of Galatians 3:13 and, hence, of this entire portion of Galatians, is once again how he linked his interpretation to comfort and consolation. This was the hallmark of the Wittenberg Reformers' interpretation of Scripture: that the meaning of a text consisted of two parts—doctrine (definition) and its effect. When the effect of a doctrine led to despair, then, no matter how reasonable the interpretation might seem, it was still false. If the person assaulted by sin, death, terror, wrath, the devil, and evil found no consolation in a particular view of Scripture or of Christ, then there was only hell to pay and the interpretation had to be false or, rather, only law. So Luther concluded a section of his work on Galatians with these words, "With gratitude and with a sure confidence, therefore, let us accept this doctrine, so sweet and so filled with comfort, which teaches that Christ became a curse for us (that is, a sinner worthy of the wrath of God); that he clothed himself in our person, laid our sins on his own shoulders, and said, 'I have committed the sins that all people have committed.'"[86] It all came down to Paul's "for us." Once again Luther interpreted the text with a dramatic monologue, returning to the "joyous exchange" he had introduced in 1519.

By this fortunate exchange with us he took upon himself our sinful person and granted us his innocent and victorious person. Clothed

85. WA 40/1:438, 32–35; 439, 13–31; and 440, 15–16 (=LW 26:281). Luther noted the "amazing and outstanding" power of the phrase "in himself," which showed that this battle took place in Christ. WA 40/1:440, 30–33 (=LW 26:282): "If you look at this Person, therefore, you see sin, death, the wrath of God, hell, the devil, and all evils conquered and put to death. To the extent that Christ rules by his grace in the hearts of the faithful, there is no sin or death or curse."
86. WA 40/1:442, 31–34 and 443, 14 (=LW 26:283–84).

and dressed in this, we are freed from the curse of the Law, because Christ himself voluntarily became a curse for us, saying, "For my own person of humanity and divinity I am blessed, and I am in need of nothing whatever. But I shall empty myself [Phil. 2:7]; I shall take on your clothing and mask; and in this I shall walk about and suffer death, in order to set you free from death."[87]

From this Luther then derived personal comfort, addressing the reader and hearer directly. "Therefore if sin makes you anxious, and if death terrifies you, just think that this is an empty specter and an illusion of the devil—as it certainly is. For in fact there is no sin any longer, no curse, no death, and no devil, because Christ has conquered and abolished all these. Therefore, the victory of Christ is completely certain; nor is there any defect in the reality itself, which is completely true, but it is instead in our incredulity, for it is difficult for reason to believe such immeasurable good things."[88]

Luther summed up his insights into this text as follows: "Undoubtedly Paul treated these things at great length in the presence of the Galatians. For this is the proper task of the apostles: to illuminate the work and the glory of Christ and to strengthen and comfort troubled consciences."[89] This twofold project—illumining Christ's work and giving comfort (*doctrina et usus*)—was at the heart of the Wittenberg Reformers' interpretation of Scripture and stood in direct conflict not only with Jerome and Erasmus—with scholastics and Romanists—but also with our own rather tame, law-centered approaches to texts that cannot believe Paul's own radical words and prefer the safety of interpretation that leaves people to their own devices as they stare into the modern or postmodern abyss.

---

87. WA 40/1:443, 23–29 (=LW 26:284).
88. WA 40/1:444, 19–24 (=LW 26:284–85).
89. WA 40/1:451, 25–27 (=LW 26:290).

An Afterword

Looking Forward to Reading the Bible with Luther

I n 1539 Luther wrote a preface to the first volume of his German works. In it he reflected on what made a true theologian, combining an interpretation of Psalm 119 with a positive appropriation of a classic monastic approach to reading Scripture. The monks outlined a threefold method: *oratio, meditatio,* and *illuminatio* (prayer, meditation, and illumination). Luther, while taking over the first two (although in very idiosyncratic ways), changed the third to its opposite—*tentatio* (literally, "temptation," but in the German equivalent, *Anfechtung,* "assault" or "attack")—because he was convinced that when one reads Scripture all hell breaks loose. Moreover, Luther thought he detected this very method in Psalm 119, which he thought David had written and which even modern scholars claim provides a summary of the Psalms and the Torah, as did Luther. His comments, written only four years after publication of his commentary on Galatians, echoed the very approach we have found in the previous chapter and, indeed, throughout this entire book.

> I will show you a right way to study theology, which I myself have practiced and, if you adhere to it, you too shall be so learned that, if need should arise, you will be able to write books that are as good as

those of the fathers and councils. . . . It is the way that King David teaches in Psalm 119 and which was without a doubt adhered to by all the patriarchs and prophets. There you will find three rules which are abundantly set forth in the whole psalm: *oratio, meditatio, tentatio.*[1]

First, Luther claimed that a theologian had to approach the text with prayer. Yet this prayer was not the pious words of a holy person seeking richer understanding or deeper insight but rather the desperation of someone confronted by the text's very foolishness and counterrational statements.

> First, you must know that the Holy Scriptures is a book that makes foolishness of the wisdom of all other books, because none of them teaches eternal life, only this one alone. Therefore you must straightway despair of your own mind and reason, for you will not attain it by these. On the contrary, with such presumption you will cast yourself, and others with you, from heaven into the abyss of hell, as did Lucifer. Rather kneel down in your closet and pray to God in true humility and earnestness, that through his dear Son he may grant you his Holy Spirit to enlighten, guide, and give you understanding. You see how David in the above-mentioned psalm prays again and again: Teach me! O Lord, instruct me! Show me! and many other expressions like them. Even though he knew well the text of Moses and other books and heard and read them daily, he still desires the real Master of the Scriptures himself in order that he may not tackle them with his reason and make himself the master. For this produces those sectarians who allow themselves to think that the Scriptures are subject to them and easily mastered with their own reason, as if they were the fables of Markolf or Aesop, which require neither the Holy Spirit nor prayer.[2]

Then, Luther moved to meditation. Yet here too he emphasized not mystical reverie or intellectual prowess but a kind of amazement with the specific words in a scriptural passage. Far from providing a spiritual springboard to higher thoughts, the biblical text drove one to consider why the Holy Spirit said this specific thing.

1. John Doberstein, ed. and trans., *A Minister's Prayer Book: An Order of Prayers and Readings* (Philadelphia: Muhlenberg, 1959), 287. See also LW 34:279–88 for a different translation.
2. Doberstein, *A Minister's Prayer Book*, 287–88.

Second, you should meditate, not only in your heart but also outwardly, repeating and comparing the actual, literal words in the book, reading and rereading them with careful attention and thought as to what the Holy Spirit means by them. And guard against being satiated or thinking that when you have read, heard, or said it once or twice you understand it fully; for this will never make an excellent theologian; it will be like immature fruit that falls before it is half ripe. This is why in the psalm you see David constantly exulting that he would do nothing else, day and night and always, but speak, write, utter, sing, hear, and read God's Word and commandments. For God will not give you his Spirit apart from the external word. Be guided accordingly, for it was not for nothing that he commanded that his Word should be outwardly written, preached, read, sung, and spoken.[3]

Finally, the result of such a prayerful, careful reading of Scripture led not to contemplation or illumination but to attack: *tentatio*, the Latin equivalent of *Anfechtung* (assault). Even today people do not want to hear that Scripture overturns their reasonable assumptions, which explains why Luther's approach to the Bible still upsets the (self-)righteous and why it comforts the sinner. Here again Luther moves from definition to effect.

Thirdly, there is *tentatio* (attack [*Anfechtung*]). This is the touchstone that teaches you not only to know and understand but also to experience how right, how true, how sweet, how lovely, how mighty, how comforting is God's Word, wisdom above all wisdom. So you see why it is that David so often in this psalm laments concerning all the enemies, the wicked princes and tyrants, the lying and godless spirits, which he must suffer by reason of the very fact that he meditates, that he applies himself to God's Word, as we have said. For as soon as God's Word goes forth through you the devil will afflict you and make you a real doctor [of theology] and teach you by his attacks to seek and to love God's Word. For I myself . . . must be very thankful to my papists for pummeling, pressing, and terrifying me; that is, for making me a fairly good theologian, for otherwise I would not have become one. . . . So there you have David's rule. If you study well according to this example, you will also sing and praise with him in the

3. Ibid., 288.

words of the same psalm: "The law of thy mouth is better to me than thousands of gold and silver pieces."[4]

One can only marvel at Luther's ability to extrude meaning from the biblical text, as we have seen not only in his interpretations of Galatians sampled in chapter 5 but in the earlier chapters as well. Instead of resolving or domesticating the paradoxes he found in Scripture, Luther reveled in them and took their very unsettling nature as the point. Paul wished to turn his readers upside down in order to flummox their reason and drive them to faith. For Luther three things converged to make sense of the Pauline arguments: the conviction that meaning converged in definition and effect (law and gospel); the even-greater conviction that the paradoxical nature of the text brought about the death of the old, reasonable creature (theology of the cross); and the experience of the God who justifies the ungodly. The text authorizes itself by producing faith in the hearer. This prevented Luther from reading texts lifelessly (*frigide*) and drove him to find methods that enlivened the text itself to his audience. To bring about this enlivening, the rigors of the scholastic method—with its countless divisions according to Aristotelian logic and solutions to contradictions using the same logic—spelled for him only *rigor mortis*, reason's last gasps at trying to deflect the judgment of the law and the scandal of the cross and domesticate it into terms acceptable to human willing and doing. Instead, God, the law, and Paul himself must speak a word. The imagery of the crucified Christ as substitute or victor—or, frankly, anything else—must finally confront the reader from out of the text itself. Most importantly, interpreters dare not eliminate the foolishness and paradox of the text but heighten them until they do their worst (terror) and best (comfort) to the hearer.

The domestication of the biblical text—practiced in concert by the most liberal and the most conservative exegetes (and most everyone in between)—poses the single greatest threat to the biblical message and its authority today. The Bible can hardly authenticate or authorize itself when interpreters insist on excusing God and interring God's Word in some historical or logical grave or another. Paul, the

4. Ibid., 288–89 (translation modified).

untimely born witness to the resurrected One, cannot be reduced to fiddling with the ceremonial law to make it more palatable to Gentile Christians any more than Jesus' breaking of the Sabbath was simply about changing customs from worshiping on Saturday to worshiping on Sunday. Human existence itself is at stake. Only when one is forced to abandon the quaint question popular among Luther's Reformed and Roman contemporaries ("Am I a sheep or am I a goat?") for the terrifying question of human existence ("Is God carnivorous or herbivorous?") do today's readers of Scripture stand a chance of hearing, let alone proclaiming, the remarkable, life-giving answer: God kills to make alive; God dies to make alive.[5] Finally, what the Word produces—believers—is in essence its authority (*auctoritas*).

Then too good, moral works are simply fruits of faith, not its justification. The Word, and the preaching and proclamation of it, produces good trees—that is, believers, people who trust God alone. Then, instead of "works of the law" a believer produces "fruits of the Spirit." Or, rather, the Spirit-filled Word creates both believing trees and their good fruit. Imitation of Christ or the law does not make God's sons or daughters; instead, affiliation—adoption as sons and daughters—makes imitators. Yet for Luther—unlike countless well-meaning preachers of every denomination who inhabit the pulpits of our Sunday assemblies each week in today's world—the point of proclamation is *never* the fruit but always the making of believers, always drawing people to the center of the gospel: God in Christ reconciling the world to himself. In this, Luther is a voice in the wilderness, pointing to Christ and proclaiming him alone to be "the Lamb of God who takes away the sin of the world." All who have ears to hear, let them hear!

---

5. The image comes from Stephen Ozment according to a comment made by David Steinmetz.

Subject Index

Scripture Index